Thou Shalt Not Speak My Language

Middle East Literature in Translation
Michael Beard and Adnan Haydar, *Series Editors*

✤ Other titles in Middle East Literature in Translation

Thou Shalt Not Speak My Language

Abdelfattah Kilito

Translated from the Arabic by Waïl S. Hassan

pou Mary
bien amicalement
Abdelfattah Kilito

SYRACUSE UNIVERSITY PRESS

English translation copyright © 2008 by Syracuse University Press
Syracuse, New York 13244-5160

All Rights Reserved

First Edition 2008
08 09 10 11 12 13   6 5 4 3 2 1

Originally published in Arabic as *Lan tatakalama lughati* (Beirut: Dar al-tali'a, 2002).

The paper used in this publication meets the minimum requirements of American National Standard for Information Sciences—Permanence of Paper for Printed Library Materials, ANSI Z39.48–1984.∞™

For a listing of books published and distributed by Syracuse University Press, visit our Web site at SyracuseUniversityPress.syr.edu.

ISBN-13: 978-0-8156-3191-0   ISBN-10: 0-8156-3191-X

Library of Congress Cataloging-in-Publication Data

Kilito, Abdelfattah, 1945–
[Lan tatakallama lughati. English]
Thou shalt not speak my language / Abdelfattah Kilito ; translated from the Arabic by Waïl S. Hassan.— 1st ed.
p. cm.
Includes bibliographical references.
ISBN 978-0-8156-3191-0 (cloth : alk. paper)
1. Arabic literature—Miscellanea.   I. Hassan, Waïl S.   II. Title.
PJ7515.K5813 2008
892.7—dc22
2008022410

Contents

Abdelfattah Kilito is a professor in the Department of French at Muhammad V University in Rabat, Morocco, and has published extensively on Arabic literature, writing in both French (most recently, *Les mille et une nuits: du texte au mythe* [The Thousand and One Nights: From Text to Myth, 2005]) and Arabic (*Al-Adab wa al-irtiyab* [Literature and Doubt, 2007]). He has been a visiting scholar at the École des Hautes Études en Science Sociales, the Collège de France, and Harvard University. In 1989 he was awarded the Grand Prix du Maroc.

Waïl S. Hassan is an associate professor of comparative literature at the University of Illinois at Urbana-Champaign. He is the author of *Tayeb Salih: Ideology and the Craft of Fiction.*

Translator's Introduction

Abdelfattah Kilito is one of Morocco's and the Arab world's most original literary critics. He is the author, in Arabic and French, of many books on classical Arabic literature, of which *L'auteur et ses doubles* (1985) has been published by Syracuse University Press as *The Author and His Doubles*. The present volume was first published in Arabic in 2002 under the title *Lan tatakalama lughati*. It is a book about the politics of language, bilingualism, translation, and cross-cultural relations, and it puts on full display that rare ability to bring startling insights into otherwise familiar texts that Kilito's readers have come to expect. As its title intimates, the book leaves few common—and commonsense—assumptions unchallenged. By turns persuasive and provocative, controversial and conclusive, it disrupts dominant modes of Arabic literary scholarship and challenges us, in the United States, to reexamine contemporary notions of translation, bilingualism, postcoloniality, the pedagogy of world literature, and the discipline of comparative literature.

Arab readers, scholars, and critics, to whom the book is specifically addressed, are heirs to two cultural traditions: the Arabic tradition of religious and humanistic learning that stretches from the fifth century to the present and includes the various branches of Islamic studies as well as linguistic, historical, philosophical, and literary fields that emerged during the development of Arab civilization; and European learning, which was introduced to the Arab world in the nineteenth century. Unlike past Arab cultural encounters with Greek, Persian, and Indian cultures, the relationship between Arab and European traditions since the colonial era has been fraught with anxiety, as Kilito illustrates in the preface and in his discussion of Orientalist scholarship in chapter 1. That does not mean, of course, that earlier encounters were free of tension, productive and otherwise, as we learn in chapters 2 and 3. Kilito foregrounds the problem of cultural translation as an interpretive process, as a pedagogical strategy, and as a methodological imperative in transnational and comparative literary studies and goes on, in brilliant readings of al-Jahiz, Ibn Rushd, Ibn Battuta, al-Saffar, and al-Shidyaq, among others, to trace the shifts in attitude toward language and translation from the centuries of Arab cultural ascendancy to the contemporary period, interrogating along the way the process by which cultural hegemony perpetuates itself.

Kilito's method consists of focusing on significant turning points in Arab cultural history from the ninth to the nineteenth century, and through close readings of carefully selected passages from canonical and lesser-known texts, identifying the dialectics that structure them. In the prologue and first chapter, he highlights the paradoxes of Arab-European literary relations in the modern period. Then he takes us back, in chapter 2, to the ninth century, at the height of Arab civilization, where we find al-Jahiz in the middle of ethnic controversies and unable to compose a book because his writings constantly turn in two directions: Arabs and Persians, literature and philosophy, translatability and untranslatability. In chapter 3, we encounter the twelfth-century philosopher Ibn Rushd (Averroës) at work interpreting Aristotle but unable to understand the *Poetics* in

Matta ibn Yunus's Arabic translation. In chapter 4, the four-teenth-century Moroccan traveler Ibn Battuta is likewise caught in a dialectic of movement and stillness that defines his relationship to language, power, and spirituality. In the following two chapters, we find two nineteenth-century Arab travelers to Europe for whom the shift in the balance of power between Arabs and Europeans spells a profound cultural crisis and puts into question the relationship between the past, the present, and the future. Chapter 7 links the dualities of gender, language, and translation to sexual politics and twentieth-century global geopolitics. The epilogue rounds off the argument by underlining the normalized absurdity of some reigning attitudes in the field of Arabic literary scholarship.

This approach allows Kilito to put standard interpretations of classical texts into question; indeed, one of the most frequent gestures in the book is to raise questions that are in turn methodological, pedagogical, or rhetorical. At times, his rhetorical questions express his indignation and exasperation at the persistence of Orientalist modes of scholarship. For instance, in exposing the hegemonic assumptions of Eurocentric comparativism, he asks what happens when we apply to Dante Charles Pellat's absurd approach to al-Maʿarri, whose *Risalat al-ghufran* is often compared to *The Divine Comedy*. Or when he wonders, in the epilogue, whether Matta ibn Yunus's mistranslation of Aristotle's *Poetics* benefited rather than harmed Arabic literature, Kilito exposes conscious and unconscious biases perpetuated by Orientalists and their Arab followers—the former out of smug condescension, the latter out of internalized inferiority.

At the heart of Kilito's project is his preoccupation with the ethics of translation. Arabic has two words for "translation": *tarjamah* means "biography" or "life," an important genre in classical Arabic scholarship, as well as "explanation in another language" and "interpretation." A translator is a *mutarjim* or a *turjuman*. As *Lisan al-'arab* and Lane's *Dictionary* indicate, *tarjamah* shares the root verb *rajama*, which means "to stone to death," with a sizeable constellation of words that include *rajm* (killing, beating, battering, reviling), *rajam* (well, cavity, hole in the ground, oven), *rujm* (shooting stars), *rajeem* (cast with stones, damned, an epithet of Satan, and also driven away, reviled, insulted), *rujmah* (grave and tombstones). The verb *rajama* also appears in expressions like *rajm bil-ghayb* (conjecture, soothsaying) and *kalam marjum* (uncertain or unreliable speech). *Tarjamah*, therefore, carries connotations of alienated speech that has the flavor of falsehood, damnation, and death, but also possibilities of survival, narration, and understanding. The other word, *naql*, means "to transfer," "to move," "to put in different words," and "to put into the words of another language." The English word "translation," which derives from the Latin *translatus*, past participle of *transferre*, also means "to transfer," "to move from one place to another," and "to carry across." The French word *traduire* (from the Latin *traducere*) and the German *übersetzen* convey the same idea of moving from one place to another. *Webster's New World Dictionary* offers the following definition of the verb "translate":

> 1. to move from one place or condition to another; transfer, specif., a) *Theol.* to convey directly to heaven without death; b) *Eccles.* to transfer (a bishop) from one see to another; also, to move (a saint's body or remains) from one place of interment to another; 2. to put into the words of a different language; 3. to change into another medium or form [to *translate* ideas into action]; 4. to put into different words; rephrase or paraphrase

in explanation; 5. to transmit (a telegraphic message) again by means of automatic relay; 6. [Archaic] to enrapture; entrance; 7. *Mech.* to impart translation to.

This definition suggests that translation hovers on the boundary between life and death, between love and death. Thus, to transfer a saint directly to heaven without death is translation, as is the transfer of a dead saint's remains from one tomb to another. To translate is also to enrapture, to transport, to entrance through love, both sacred and profane.

Life and death, love and war, are seemingly contrasting metaphors that fuse in the potent representation of the Greek god Eros, who inflicts love through an instrument of death. Eros, therefore, is an *arch* translator insofar as he represents translation not only as a violent process that alters its object but also as a circular one in which love and death dovetail. We might say that, in translation, Eros merges with Thanatos. Eros's arrows conjure up a classic image of love, namely that of the hunt, which we find in Imru'ul-Qays, Petrarch, and Shakespeare, among others, and which is vividly captured in Thomas Wyatt's sonnet that begins, "Whoso list to hunt, I know where is an hind." The playful angelic boy turns into an aggressive adult who relentlessly and ruthlessly chases, shoots, and kills a deer in the name of sport. In the masculinist imaginary that produces the poetic convention and its inexorable division of sexual labor, the hunter is always male, the hunted female; needless to say, the breaking of convention is highly conventional, as Kilito demonstrates in chapters 6 and 7. Regardless of who the hunter is and who the prey, courtship on this model is a violent conquest, and the fulfillment of love is death both for the hunted, in the logic of the metaphor, and of the hunter, in the poetic translation of orgasmic expiration. In the absence noted by Walter Benjamin of a muse of translation, theorists have tended to privilege either Eros or Thanatos as a patron of the neglected art in their effort to define an ethics of translation. The two positions appear contradictory, but it is my contention that such an ethics is possible if the two are held together in productive tension.

Broadly speaking, translation encompasses the extremes of radical transformation, expressed in metaphors of heightened life and afterlife—that is, metaphors of altered states. From the translator's perspective, original states are considered deficient and unsatisfactory, and translation purports to remedy this fallen state of texts through the work of supplementation. Benjamin's often-quoted comment on translation as the afterlife of the original owes much to this conception of the Babelic state of texts (Benjamin 1968, 71). "Afterlife" suggests that the original is doomed to oblivion and irrelevance unless translation gives it new life. On that theory, the task of the translator, in one sense at least, is to allow the original to speak to another audience, from beyond the grave of another time or another language. Of course, the translator is no passive or transparent *medium*, contrary to quasi-spiritualist notions of translation. Rather, I would say, the translator is more of a ventriloquist, an interpreter who, from a highly determined discursive and ideological position (conscious or unconscious, acknowledged or unacknowledged), makes texts of the past or of another language speak to the here and now, or, more radically, who speaks about the here and now through those texts. In the Derridean logic of the supplement, translation does not just complete or complement the original but in the process finishes it off. If the pre-Babelian state of linguistic wholeness is no more than a nostalgic myth of origin, then original and translation are not matching "fragments of a greater language," as Benjamin puts it (1968, 78)—even if no gathering of such fragments will ever restore the original wholeness of language, as Paul de Man argues (de Man 1986, 91)—but antagonists vying for supremacy over one another. Translation tries to evict and displace the original, while the original ever tries to render translation impossible—and Kilito offers al-Hariri's *maqamat* as an example of that. In the extreme, translation becomes a species of cannibalism whereby the translator consumes the original text, at once eliminating it and absorbing its power.

It has been said that the difference between a dialect and a language is that a language is a dialect with an army. It follows that surviving dialects must remain subordinated to dominant languages, deprived of writing, literature, national flags, and armies. It also follows that some languages have stronger armies than others. The question of what happens in the translation of texts from languages with weaker armies into ones with greater military might has been given much deserved attention in recent translation studies in the United States, a country that possesses the most powerful military in history. In some cases, translation functions as the extension of military, political, and economic power, much the same way that Orientalism has facilitated and justified imperialism. In that sense, some languages prey on others, colonize them, plunder and cannibalize their texts. When it does not fulfill culturally imperialist purposes, translation serves commercial, strategic, or military interests. Witness, for example, U.S. government support for Russian and Soviet studies during the Cold War and the crisis such programs faced in the 1990s when that support ended, and the current exponential expansion, for similar reasons, of Arabic language programs. The story of area studies since World

War II reflects this ebb and flow of foreign policy priorities, for which language study and translation are purely instrumental: their logic is that of "Know your enemy!"

Of course, there are also other sorts of translation that result from openness to, and even admiration for, certain cultures perceived as rich or as worthy of dialogue with our own. Which cultures are so perceived, which not, and why, are revealing albeit rarely asked questions. To some extent, the history of literary studies and literary pedagogy in the United States over the past four decades can be told as a narrative of the contested expansion of that dialogic circle. The so-called theory revolution in literary studies, the interrogation of the canon and attendant liberalization of college curricula to include women's, minority, Asian, African, and Latin American traditions, the rise of postcolonial studies, the more recent prominence of translation studies, and the ongoing efforts to reconfigure the discipline of comparative literature, are all efforts in that direction.

The heated debates over the politics of language in postcolonial writing during the early decades of decolonization centered on the same concern with conflict and cultural hegemony and emancipation. In that context, Kilito's Moroccan compatriot Abdelkebir Khatibi went beyond Chinua Achebe's argument that Africans can appropriate the colonizers' language, Africanize it, and make it their own. Khatibi theorized the encounter between the languages of colonizer and colonized as the erotics of an *"amour bilingue."* Bilingual love begets a hybridized offspring, a language semantically infused by its Other, bearing the marks of linguistic and ideological contamination. Likewise Israeli-Palestinian writer, critic, and translator Anton Shammas, who writes in Arabic and Hebrew, asserts that "writing in any language, even that of the colonizer, is a form of love" (1988,

163; my translation)—although he differentiates his own situation as a multilingual writer who enjoys the freedom to choose his medium from the predicament of some Maghrebian writers on whom French was imposed by a colonial system that proscribed Arabic literacy. Shammas's deliberate choice of Hebrew over Arabic in his novel *Arabesques* afforded him a certain artistic freedom (to write about family members in a language foreign to them), imposed on him a productive linguistic discipline (the cautious precision of a nonnative speaker), and also allowed him discursively to divorce the Hebrew language from Zionist ideology that conflates language, ethnicity, and nationhood, enabling him, as a non-Jewish Israeli citizen, to stake a claim to the language (Siddiq 2000, 163–64). Writing in Hebrew or French allows writers like Shammas and Khatibi to elope with the colonizers' language, to dissociate it from the ideologies of Zionism and *la mission civilisatrice*. This love perverts the colonizers' language, making it serve anticolonial ends.

A rigorously self-conscious conception of ethical agency governs the passage from bilingual love to love in translation. Reverence for the "original" correlates that ethical imperative with the ecclesiastical sense of "translation" in *Webster's* definition, for to "translate" a saint's remains requires elaborate rituals, the purpose of which is to sanctify the act and to ward off the evil consequences of sacrilege. In the same vein, as Douglas Robinson shows, the translation of sacred texts was for millennia considered taboo, to be undertaken only by high priests on special occasions, such as initiation into divine mysteries. Such initiation radically transforms the initiate, who must be willing to surrender himself or herself to the divine power unleashed through translation. Robinson identifies a paradigmatic case in Lucius Apuleius's *The Golden Ass*, which involves multiple

metamorphoses of the protagonist, culminating with his initiation into the cult of Isis (Robinson 1996, 3–45). Delineating a
notion of literary translation that, in its respect for the original
and emphasis on the transformative potential of translation,
functions as a secular equivalent to Robinson's, Gayatri Spivak
invokes Luce Irigaray's discussion of the place of love in ethics
to describe literary translation as "the most intimate act of reading." Spivak argues that the translator must "surrender to the
text" in order to "solicit the text to show the limits of its language" (Spivak 1993, 183). Through that surrender, the translator "earns permission to transgress from the trace of the other"
(180). Echoing Khatibi's metaphor of *amour bilingue*, Spivak
argues that "the task of the translator is to facilitate this love
between the original and its shadow, a love that permits fraying,
holds the agency of the translator and the demands of her imagined or actual audience at bay. The politics of translation from a
non-European woman's text too often suppresses this possibility
because the translator cannot engage with, or cares insufficiently
for, the rhetoricity of the original" (181). In extreme cases, this
kind of translation forges a text that reproduces the dominant
ideology of the target culture—for instance, dominant Western
representations of Muslim woman, as Amal Amireh and Mohja
Kahf have demonstrated in their studies of the English translations of Nawal al-Sadaawi and Huda Sha'rawi, respectively.
Such beating into shape of the original shares an etymological
root with forgery (Latin *fabricare*). Translation becomes a species
of forgery or sacrilege when, in Spivak's metaphor, transgression
or deviation from the letter of the original, which is the condition of all translation, is not authorized by an ethics of "fraying,"
that is, "a disrupting, yet 'loving' rhetoricity that enters into the
text's self-staging rather than searches for synonym, syntax, and

local color" (Apter 2006, 102); or in the case of sacrilege, without ritual sanction or when intentional desecration occurs.[1]

These notions of forgery and sacrilege take center stage in Kilito's conception of bilingualism and translation. If for Spivak epistemic violence often governs the translation of non-European women's texts into English, for Kilito, it is the condition of all translation. His book *The Author and His Doubles* revolves around the phenomenon of literary forgery, and *Thou Shalt Not Speak My Language* posits bilingualism as a species of mortal sin. Kilito invokes al-Jahiz's comparison of bilingualism to polygamy, which entails that the relationship between languages "meeting on one tongue" is one of jealous rivalry and hostility. Al-Jahiz's theory of bilingualism developed in the context of the ethnic tensions known as *shuʻubiyyah* that marked early Abbasid politics. Finding in it a historical referent from within Arab intellectual history that speaks to the modern (post)colonial predicament of North Africa, Kilito argues that any linguistic encounter involves a contest over dominance that he depicts in images of warfare. In *The Author and His Doubles*, he asserts:

> When two languages live side by side, one or the other will always appear bestial. If you do not speak as I do, you are an animal. The "I" in this case must occupy the dominant position; if I am the weaker party, it is I who am the animal. To call this situation a conflict is incorrect, because conflict requires adversaries of equal or at least comparable strength. A lion may battle a tiger, but he simply devours a rabbit. Bilingualism

1. The two preceding paragraphs are lightly revised and reproduced here for their relevance to the present discussion from my article "Agency and Translational Literature: Ahdaf Soueif's *The Map of Love*," *PMLA* 121, no. 3 (May): 753–68.

does not evoke an image of two gladiators advancing upon each other armed with nets and tridents; rather, it suggests that one of the two combatants is already sprawled in the dust awaiting the fatal blow. (2001, 108)

Kilito here contests Khatibi's metaphor of bilingual love by giving us two alternative metaphors: in the first one, instead of eroticism there is bestiality, and in the second, instead of love we find combat, conquest, and bloodshed. Either way, bilingualism represents not the mutual enrichment of languages, but the annihilation of one by the other. The lion devours the rabbit and battles the tiger. Powerful languages fight each other to the death, whereas stronger languages simply eradicate weaker ones.

We may, of course, protest the efficacy of this logic on several grounds, wondering for instance why bilingualism is categorically posited in terms of violence, although this should also lead us to ask why bilingualism should likewise be categorically explained in terms of love by Khatibi and others. Kilito's Darwinian fatalism is the answer to Khatibi's utopianism. Still, Kilito does not explain why there are still so many languages left, or how some rabbits have tried, with a measure of success, to escape from the lion's jaws. Many languages have survived colonial hegemony and emerged stronger. While some languages were indeed vanquished—for example, Breton and Langue d'Oc in France—Arabic reasserted itself in North Africa, and several sub-Saharan African languages acquired armies and writing systems and became national languages.

Further, one could take issue with Kilito's choice of animals: why should bilingualism be more fittingly depicted as a lion devouring a rabbit rather than a lion battling a tiger? Or for that matter, why not posit languages as animals of the same species, as linguists, anthropologists, and philosophers of language might object? Or we may argue with the naturalization implied in the use of animal imagery to begin with, which normalizes attitudes of essentialism, cultural nationalism, and monolingual chauvinism. Besides, is not the use of language one of the decisive, if not *the* decisive, differences between humans and animals? If Kilito's argument is informed by the (post)colonial context of the Maghreb, what about other kinds of bilingualism?

Nevertheless, Kilito's argument is valid as the embodiment of colonial desire and an articulation of the ideology of conquest. Those who speak another language are, ipso facto, not animals, but that did not stop the Greeks from calling others barbarians, implying their subhumanity, or the pre-Islamic Arabians from describing non-Arabs as *'ajam* (literally, without intelligible speech, also an attribute of animals). Likewise, the French ideology of assimilation held out the carrot of humanity and civilization to the natives precisely through the French language. That many—not all—of the natives refused to be rabbits does not negate colonial desire so much as confirm it. Their refusal has not undone the ideology of assimilation but brought it into crisis, as the 2005 riots in France bear witness. In that sense, Kilito's theory of bilingualism is a sobering reminder of the realities of power.

Bilingualism has played a particularly important and complex role in Arab-Islamic civilization. The sacred book of Islam is, from the perspective of the faithful, untranslatable because it is considered the literal Word of God; human beings are incapable of exhausting its meaning, let alone transposing it into other languages. And yet the first word of the Qur'an to be revealed was "*iqra*," which means both "recite" and "read." The first meaning refers to orality, while the second, emphasized by the illiterate prophet's response to the angel Gabriel ("*Ma ana biqari*'," that is,

"I am no reader" [al-Tabari 1984, 15: 251]), points to literacy. In a predominantly oral culture in which only the most important documents were written down, to take this initial divine command literally meant reading books in other languages. That is precisely what the Arabs did in the early centuries of Islam, when they translated copiously from Persian, Sanskrit, Syriac, Greek, and other languages. Two well-known hadiths attributed to the prophet encouraged the learning of other languages: "Seek knowledge though it be in China" (the remotest developed civilization at the time), and "Whoever learns the language of another people safeguards against their evil scheming." Bilingualism here is both an avenue to learning and a security imperative; at the same time, the sacred language of Islam retains its exalted position at the center of cultural and spiritual life. That some scholars have dispute the authenticity of those hadiths is all the more indicative of the partisan battles fought over the relative worth of different languages and the value of bilingualism.[2] Needless to say, it was ethnic and linguistic tensions that occasioned the polemics reported by al-Jahiz, as Kilito explains in chapter 2, but even in Islamic states where other languages were dominant (Persia, Mughal India, Ottoman Turkey), the Arabic language and Arab scholars enjoyed a special prestige that explains Ibn Battuta's relatively easy access to Muslim kings outside of the Arab world, and his corresponding lack of access to Arab potentates, as Kilito points out in chapter 4.

Colonialism disrupted that linguistic order, especially in the Maghreb, where French was imposed and Arabic proscribed, a

---

2. Ali Hassan Ali Al-Halabi, Ibrahim Taha Qaysi, and Hamdi Muhammad Murad, *Mawsu'at al-ahadith wa al-athar al-da'ifa wa al-mawdu'a* (Riyadh: Maktabat al-ma'arif li al-nashr wa al-tawzi', 1999).

situation that set the stage for Kilito's warfare metaphors and his preoccupation with colonial bilingualism. In *Thou Shalt Not Speak My Language*, Kilito's arguments seem counterintuitive: we inhabit language, but we fight against it; bilingualism is the result of (and, to complete the vicious circle, it brings about) violence and antagonism rather than peaceful coexistence; the role of the bilingual as cultural translator is doomed to failure, and a good thing, too. Such sentiments substantiate the following striking confession in chapter 7:

> One day I realized that I dislike having foreigners speak my language. How did that happen? I used to think of myself as an open-minded, liberal person who wished unto others what he wished unto his kin; furthermore, I used to think it my duty to endeavor as best I could to make my language "radiate" its brilliance, to work to increase the number of its learners, and so forth. But that noble goal disappeared when I realized that I dislike having foreigners speak my language. That dislike had actually been there all along, except that I had not been aware of it and dared not confess it to myself, let alone to others.

Again, there is conflict, but is it no longer just between two languages; it is also between the liberal belief in promoting cross-cultural understanding through language learning, and a secret, obscene, jealous desire to possess one's native language so completely as to prevent others from using it for their purposes, which can only be perverse and dishonorable. This sense is reinforced on the back cover of Kilito's Arabic text, where the above confession is reproduced followed by this sentence, which is not found inside the book: "But now I reveal it [that is, his dislike for having others speak his language] to the reader, and to those concerned with Arabic culture, so that we may ponder how they have treated Arabic and the other languages." Kilito's statement here pertains explicitly to the Arabic language and its treatment by European Orientalists, the subject of chapter 1, which could have been entitled "How Not to Do Comparative Literature." Some Arab scholars have also internalized and reproduced Orientalist attitudes that still shape Arabic literary scholarship today, as the epilogue shows. Kilito's secret wish, therefore, bespeaks a counterhegemonic impulse to defend Arabic against the attempts of Orientalists to devour the rabbit, and self-Orientalizing Arabs who volunteer to season it to taste. The title of the book at once bans the voracious gluttony of colonial bilingualism in the biblical language of prohibition ("Thou shalt not speak my language"), and predicts its failure to turn its victim into lunch ("No matter how hard you try, you will never be able to speak my language as I do").

This second meaning is comforting only up to a point: until it is challenged by the uncanny figure of the foreigner who indeed speaks our language with perfect pitch. In chapter 7, Kilito gives three examples to illustrate this uncanniness, which springs from the fear of losing one's "last place of refuge," one's identity, to foreigners. The first example comes from a detective novel by American writer Donna Leon, *Death at La Fenice*, in which an Italian detective meets a foreigner whose Italian seems to equal the detective's; the second comes from a German account of an incident that took place in China; and the third is a personal anecdote about a foreign student whose command of the Moroccan dialect surprised and embarrassed Kilito. There are at least three interesting facts about those examples. First, the uncanniness turns out to be common to the speakers of Arabic as well as of other languages, and not only confined to (post) colonial situations. Second, attitudes to language are highly gendered. Third, in the first and third instances, and as a reflection of male anxiety and current geopolitics, the usurper of language, the foreign invader, the self-proclaimed lion to the native speaker's rabbit, is significantly an American woman. Kilito's analysis of the sexual tension and its linguistic dimension leads him to question the nostalgia for the lost paradise of linguistic identity and wholeness.

In those examples, bilingualism is caught up in a battle of the sexes in which attraction is inextricably mixed with the desire for domination, both at the personal and the geopolitical levels. Bilingualism and translation are steeped in the anxiety that defines the erotic as a tension between surrender and conquest, although it is never clear, at any given moment, who the hunter is and who the prey. Thus while at first glance the book appears to be a manifesto for cultural nationalism and isolationism, it in effect lays bare the anxiety at the root of chauvinism. Kilito's argument follows a polemical strategy of a Swiftian order, for the real drift of his modest proposal to ban bilingualism is a call for an ethics of translation that seems to have eluded Arabic studies so far. If the emphasis on love seems utopian at a time when the crusader language of the "clash of civilizations" and the "war on terror" has polarized public discourse in many parts of the world, Kilito's intervention challenges us, in the U.S. context, to interrogate the production of knowledge in Middle East and area studies, the pedagogy of world literature, and the role of comparative literature and the multicultural curriculum in disseminating cultural literacy.

+ + +

The Arabic title, *Lan tatakalama lughati*, is deliberately ambiguous and could be understood as either declarative or imperative, a factual statement or an Eleventh Commandment. The title of chapter 7 complicates the situation further by compounding variations on the book's title: "*La tatakalam lughati wa lan tatakallamaha.*" The first part, *La tatakalam lughati*, can itself be read in two ways: "Do not speak my language," or "You do not speak my language." The second part, "*wa lan tatakallamaha,*" means "and you will not speak it," which also supports two interpretations: "you will not be able to speak my language in the future [even if you tried]" and "you are not allowed to speak my language." In my estimation, using the archaic forms of the second person pronoun and the corresponding verb forms in the translation of both titles captures this ambiguity better than simply saying "You Will Not Speak My Language," especially given the theological evocations indicated above.

In Arabic, as in French, all nouns are gendered. *Lughah* (language) is a linguistic feminine, while *lisan* (tongue) is masculine. The implications are not lost on al-Jahiz, al-Shidyaq, or Kilito, whose discourses are nuanced in gendered ways. In order to convey some of those nuances in translation, I have retained the use of gendered pronouns whenever possible; for example, "language" is sometimes referred to as "she," and "he" is preferred to the more politically correct (but in this context inaccurate) "he or she" and "they."

In similar vein, when referring to dates, I have used "A.D." whenever Kilito refers to the Christian calendar and elsewhere instead of the currently more accepted C.E. (Common Era); to follow the logic of Kilito's argument in chapter 1 is to ask, "common to who?" "A.H." (after the *hijrah*) is used whenever Kilito refers to the Islamic calendar.

In transcribing Arabic words and names, I have followed a simplified version of the system used by the *International Journal of Middle East Studies*, without diacriticals. Exceptions to that practice are in observance of the manner in which some words and names are spelled in cited published translations (hence, for example, "shaikh" rather than "shaykh" in H. A. R. Gibb's translation of Ibn Battuta, or the more common "sheikh"; "as-Saffar" instead of "al-Saffar" and "Koran" in Susan Miller's translation of as-Saffar, but "Qur'an" elsewhere).

With few exceptions, I have quoted from published English translations of primary sources cited by Kilito. English-language sources are quoted directly. Quotes from French and German appear in my translation unless otherwise noted.

◆ ◆ ◆

Completion of this translation was aided in part by a Mellon Faculty Fellowship from the College of Liberal Arts and Sciences and an Arnold A. Beckman research award from the Research Board of the University of Illinois at Urbana-Champaign. It is a great pleasure to acknowledge a debt of gratitude to Mary Selden Evans for her enthusiasm and support for this project; Roger Allen for facilitating it at a crucial early stage; my research assistant Junjie Luo for able, meticulous, enthusiastic, and thorough research; William M. Calder III, R. Scott Garner, and David Sansone for giving me the benefit of their expertise in Greek culture; to Willem Floor, Rajeev Kinra, John Perry, Mohammad Yahaghi, and Zohreh Sullivan for their help with Persian; Muhammad al-Faruque for his help with the Arabic collection at the University of Illinois library and for guiding my research in electronic databases in Arabic; Ferial Ghazoul, Shaden Tageldin, Zahr Said Stauffer, Mohja Kahf, and Ibtissam Bouachrine for valuable comments on an early version of the introduction presented at the 2005 MLA convention in Washington, D.C.; Stephanie Hilger for a rigorous and astute reading of the full-length version of the introduction;

and Abdelfattah Kilito for his generous encouragement, his perpetual readiness to answer my questions, and for revising the entire manuscript twice and diplomatically correcting some of my (alas!) many errors.

Thou Shalt Not Speak My Language

I entreat you in the name of grace . . . not, in whatever concerns me, to take any measure of your Arabs, just as though they did not exist. I hate that entire race. I know that Greece produced learned, eloquent men: philosophers, poets, orators, mathematicians, all came from there. The fathers of medicine were born there, too. But Arab physicians! . . . You must know what they are. As for me, I know their poets. One cannot imagine anything feebler, more disturbing, more obscene. . . . I can hardly be made to believe that any good could come from the Arabs. Nevertheless, you, learned scholars, from what weakness I know not, heap undeserved praise upon them, so much so that I heard one physician say to his assenting colleagues that if he were to find Hippocrates's equal among the moderns, he would allow him to write only if the Arabs had written nothing. These are words which, I will not say burned in my heart . . . , but pierced it like a dagger, and would have been enough to induce me to throw all my books into the fire. . . . What! Cicero could become an orator after Demosthenes, Virgil a poet after Homer, Titus Livius and Sallustius historians after Herodotus and Thucydides, and after the Arabs no one should be allowed to write! . . . We may often equal, and occasionally surpass, the Greeks, and therefore all nations, except for the Arabs, as you say! O madness! O vertigo! O benumbed or extinguished genius of Italy!

—Petrarch

Prologue

Rare is the Arab reader who has not, at one point in his life, been influenced by Mustafa Lutfi al-Manfaluti [1876–1924] and enamored by his writing, or shed copious tears while reading him. *Magdalin, Al-sha'ir* (The Poet), *Al-fadilah* (Virtue), *Al-nadharat* (Reflections), *Fi sabil al-taj* (For the Crown)—with few exceptions (such as "Al-hallaq al-tharthar" [The Talkative Barber]), al-Manfaluti's texts are associated with sorrow, grief, and weeping; it is no coincidence that his best-known work is titled *Al-'abarat* (The Tears). He made sadness synonymous with literature, much like Gibran Khalil Gibran. Indeed, al-Manfaluti turned sadness into a value: to be sad is to be kind and gentle, to seek what is perfect and good.

But the more infatuated the adolescent with al-Manfaluti's writing, the more repelled by it is the adult reader, who turns away from it once and for all. And when he is remembered in the company of old friends, they cannot restrain their laughter. Al-Manfaluti, who laid the foundations of what we may call the poetics of sadness, provokes only ridicule and laughter (which, at any rate, is better than the annoyance that Gibran's works induce)! The fact remains, however, that reading al-Manfaluti inspired most modern writers. Indeed, they began by imitating him, only to abrogate and turn against him later. Is there an Arab writer who has not written *against* him?

Al-Manfaluti did not speak a European language, and perhaps had no desire to learn any. For that reason, his style seems

3

derivative, steeped in tradition. Nevertheless, every one of his pages whispers the same question: how do I become European? Never stated, this question is very timidly implied in his writings. If we look closely, we could break that question down into two parts. The first part is denial and protest: how could anyone accuse me of Eurocentrism when I know only Arabic, which I write the way it was written by my predecessors in the Golden Age of Arabic prose? The second part is explanation and apology: who could deny that I have done my very best to comprehend Europe and to be faithful to it?

On the cover of his books we find his name but not the names of the French authors whose novels he "translated." He was so saturated with them that they became part of his consciousness and his being, and there was no longer any need to mention or even allude to them. Al-Manfaluti was Edmond Rostand, Bernardin de Saint-Pierre, Alexandre Dumas fils, François Coppée, Alphonse Karr, and Chateaubriand.[1] Yet he appears on the cover with his sad countenance (of course) and traditional garb—turban and cloak—and seems to ask, Aren't I an Azharite?[2]

One wonders what lies beneath that cloak. What was his underwear like? I would not have raised this question, which

---

1. Most of al-Manfaluti's works, with the exception of *Al-nadharat*, are very free adaptions or Arabizations, rather than translations, of French texts: *Magdulin* is based on Alphonse Karr's *Sous les tilleuls*; *Al-sha'ir* on Edmond Rostand's *Cyrano de Bergerac*; *Al-fadilah* on Bernardin de Saint-Pierre's *Paul et Virginie*; *Fi-sabil al-taj* on François Coppée *Pour la couronne* (translator's note).

2. The influential Islamic university in Cairo, founded in the tenth century. The distinctive turban and cloak identify the wearer as a graduate of al-Azhar (translator's note).

may seem silly, if I had not read that he was fond of European underwear. Yes, it is what those with intimate knowledge of him assert (Abu al-Anwar 1981, 69). They refer to this in passing as a humorous thing, without dwelling on its deep significance, at once farcical and tragic. European dress is al-Manfaluti's secret passion, an unspeakable secret because it clings to his body, to his being. It does not appear on the cover of his books any more than the names of the European authors he adapted.

1 ✦ In the Mirror

A few years ago, I was asked to introduce al-Hamadhani's *maqamat* to a French audience in the context of a musical event organized in the city of Strasbourg.[1] At first, I thought that would be easy: it would suffice to talk about mendicity, the main theme of the *maqamat*, and to offer general remarks about rhymed prose and rhetorical embellishments. In any event, no one would hold me to account, for my audience knows nothing about the art of the *maqamat*, or about Arabic literature, for that matter. It would be an easy audience—a lecture ending in polite applause, then each would be on his way, perhaps after a few pro forma questions and answers.

However, as time went by, I began to have doubts and it became clear to me that the task was very difficult. For instance, I could begin with the following: "Al-Hamadhani composed his *maqamat* in the fourth century . . . ," but what would the audience understand by "the fourth century"? The words evoke historical, literary, religious, and even geographical factors which would be entirely unknown to that audience.

---

1. The *maqama* (pl. *maqamat*, meaning session, assembly, or meeting) is an Arabic narrative genre that emerged in the tenth century and was still popular in the early twentieth century. Written in rhymed prose, the narratives depict the adventures of a beggar or rogue. See Kilito's *Les séances: Récits et codes culturels chez Hamadhanî et Harîrî* (Paris: Sindbad, 1983) (translator's note).

6

That being the case, I said to myself, I could simply substitute the Christian for the Islamic date, so that the opening sentence would be, "Al-Hamadhani composed his *maqamat* in the tenth century . . . " In switching to the Christian calendar, I would connect Badiʿ al-Zaman al-Hamadhani to a period known to the audience and link him to his contemporary European writers. The audience would no doubt appreciate my kind gesture, for I have learned from bitter experience that the other does not care about me unless I reached out to him. I would be unlikely to succeed in introducing Arabic literature to that audience if I did not gesture toward their literature, at least out of courtesy.

Therefore, I was convinced that I must establish some link between al-Hamadhani and European writers from that period. But then an unexpected question burst into my mind: which authors? To my surprise, I realized that I did not know a single European writer from the tenth century A.D., be it a littérateur, a theologian, or a philosopher. After a long, tedious search in dictionaries and encyclopedias, I found a single name, Roswitha,[2] that belonged to a woman who lived in Germany and composed measured dialogues in Latin and verses in praise of the emperor Otto I. Dialogue, measured prose, and praise poetry all link this Roswitha to al-Hamadhani. I was fortunate to find points of comparison that I had not suspected. Now my opening sentence became: "In the tenth century, while Roswitha crafted rhymed dialogues, al-Hamadhani composed his *maqamat*."

Yet who in the audience would have heard of Roswitha? No one. Roswitha is as alien to my audience as al-Hamadhani.

---

2. The name interested me because of its connotations: rose, life, life of the rose, the rose of life. Apparently, however, its derivation has no relationship to rose or life.

Mentioning her would not do any good; on the contrary, it would complicate matters and leave the audience resentful at what would surely seem like deliberate obscurantism masquerading as erudition.

Here we touch upon the subject of literary memory. When thinking of classical Arabic literature, I always refer to the Islamic calendar. Abu Nuwas refers me to the second century, and al-Mutanabbi to the fourth. In fact, Arabic literature, as others and I see it, consists of the pre-Islamic period and the first five centuries after the *hijrah*. If I were asked to name a poet from the following centuries—the "age of decadence"—I would be at a loss to answer. Starting with the sixth century (that is, the twelfth A.D.), things get mixed up and the picture becomes obscure and uncertain. For seven centuries, Arabic literature fell into a long, deep sleep, from which it did not awake until the thirteenth century A.H. (the nineteenth A.D.), thanks to writers like Rifa'a Rafi' al-Tahtawi and Ahmad Faris al-Shidyaq.[3]

Regardless of whether or not this view is correct (the authority is with school textbooks and literary histories), what I would like to note is that when I hear of al-Tahtawi and al-Shidyaq, my mind does not turn to the thirteenth, but to the nineteenth century. If classical Arabic literature automatically refers me to the spaciousness of the *hijrah*, modern literature spontaneously refers me to Europe as a chronology and a frame of reference.

Thus Arabic literature is subject to a double chronology. At first, and for a long time, it was tied to the Islamic calendar, then

---

3. On the problems connected with this neglected period of Arabic literature, see Roger Allen and D. S. Richards, eds., *Arabic Literature in the Post-Classical Period* (Cambridge: Cambridge University Press, 2006) (translator's note).

one day, without warning, it moved to the Christian calendar! One day, after seven centuries of recumbency, it leaped up suddenly and gracefully over six centuries, and found itself in the middle of the nineteenth century, in another age and against a different horizon. It jumped from its own calendar into another, alien one.

From this perspective, Arabic literary memory is defined by three periods: the first is clear, the second characterized by stagnation and slumber, and finally a third, lasting until now, where memory lost its bearings and plunged into another memory and another time frame.

Naturally, literary memory is different for Arabs and Europeans. In both cases, it rests on a certain foundation, a primal model, a particular conception of space and time. Obviously, European memory goes back to Athens, and Arab memory to the desert. In another respect, if we take the linguistic factor into account, Arab memory seems "longer" than European memory, stretching back fifteen centuries to the *mu'allaqat*, to al-Shanfara and Muhalhil ibn Rabi'a,[4] while that of Europeans does not exceed five centuries. For the French, for example, literature that can be read in the original begins with Villon, a fifteenth-century poet, and continues with Rabelais and Montaigne. As for medieval writers, such as Adam the Hunchback, who lived in the thirteenth century, their countrymen can only read them translated into modern French. In fact, Villon, Rabelais, and Montaigne cannot be read without extensive annotation.

---

4. Literally, "the hung ones," the *mu'allaqat* are seven odes deemed by Arabs in the pre-Islamic era to be the finest specimens of poetry. The odes were reportedly written in gold and hung on the walls of the sacred shrine in Mecca, hence their name. Al-Shanfara and Muhalhil are pre-Islamic poets not among the authors of the *mu'allaqat* (translator's note).

By contrast, Arabs find no difficulty reading Ibn al-Muqaffaʻ or al-Tawhidi. It is true that reading Abu Tammam is no easy matter, but in truth this poet seems to have been difficult even to his contemporaries, which is the reason why al-Maʻarri and al-Tibrizi later wrote commentaries on him. As is well known, written Arabic, unlike spoken Arabic, has undergone only slight and secondary changes throughout its history, so that whoever today can read Nizar Qabbani can read al-ʻAbbas ibn al-Ahnaf, and those who can read Salah ʻAbd al-Sabur can read Salih ibn ʻAbd al-Quddus, and whoever reads *Midaq Alley* can also read *The Book of the Misers*. This is a strange and amazing phenomenon, rarely encountered in other cultures.

To return to the lecture I began by mentioning. It seemed to me, given the circumstances, that the most effective way to introduce al-Hamadhani's *maqamat* would be to compare them to the picaresque novel, which was popular in Spain in the sixteenth and seventeenth centuries. So when speaking about Abu al-Fath al-Iskandari, I referred to *Lazarillo de Tormes*, a work of anonymous authorship, to Quevedo's *The Swindler*, and others. In other words, I translated the *maqamat*, not in the sense of transferring them from one language to another, but presented them as though they were picaresque novels, I transferred them into a different genre, a different literature. I undertook a *cultural translation*, so to speak.

We may regard this as a praiseworthy pedagogical operation, since it is based on a sense of openness and respect for the Other and his cultural frame of reference. Yet it became clear to me afterwards that that methodology, which is widely followed by scholars, was not innocent.

In the introduction to *Le milieu basrien et la formation de Gahiz* [The Basra Milieu and the Formation of al-Jahiz], by the

French Arabist Charles Pellat, I read the following: "In general, Arabic books produce a sense of boredom, whatever their topic, and however attractive their titles" (1953, viii). Normally, one speaks of boredom in reference to a book, or an author, or a genre, yet Pellat here issues a judgment on Arabic books "in general," not only literary ones but books in all fields of knowledge. Arab culture as a whole is boring.

Those are not the words of someone with superficial knowledge of Arab culture, but of a great teacher and specialist who devoted his life to the study of the various genres of Arabic literature, and the services he rendered in disseminating it and analyzing some of its aspects are undeniable. It is not a matter here of a brief outburst of annoyance, as sometimes happens in intimate gatherings in which one rambles and issues outrageous judgments. On the contrary, we are confronting a judgment based on deep thought and exhaustive study of primary texts. Moreover, it is a written judgment, which incurs greater responsibility, and it is found in an academic work that, from the outset, requires balance, objectivity, and great care in drawing conclusions.

At first, I was astonished by this decisive statement, especially that it lacked any ambiguity whatsoever. Nevertheless, I tried to find an explanation for it, since, at any rate, its author was honest and forthright in expressing his opinion, and that is a virtue. It is not rare that one hears readers of Arabic philosophy, for instance, whisper to one another that there is no benefit to be gained from reading al-Kindi or Ibn Sina (Avicenna), without having the courage to make their opinion public. After all, it is not a bad thing for Charles Pellat to break the consensus and say what no one else has said before or since (with the exception of Petrarch, with whose words I opened this book). This is irrespective of the amusing nature of such breaking with consensus. For instance, Don Quixote believes that he is right and that those who do not share his worldview (that is, everybody) are gravely deluded. He has gone astray, no doubt, but his delusion is tinted with truthfulness, good conscience, and dedication to high ideals and noble goals. We cannot dismiss him simply as a madman; there are those who defend him in the belief that Cervantes is less noble than him. Indeed, some believe that Don Quixote is greater than his creator.

Given those considerations, a strong doubt entered my mind. Who knows, perhaps Arabic books are boring. Like Don Quixote, Charles Pellat may be right! In what way? His stupid judgment may be worth contemplating; that is to say, it raises a question we do not often confront: how do we as Arabs see our literature, and how do we judge it?

Before tackling this issue, we must ask if Charles Pellat is alone in thinking that Arabic books are boring. Apparently, he is not alone, for he would not have allowed himself to write such a thing had he not known or felt that others share his belief. His turn of phrase indicates that he is not simply expressing a personal opinion, but one that is widespread. He is in the company of others for whom this negative judgment on Arabic writing is self-evident, unproblematic, and uncontroversial. Who are those accomplices? For whom does he write? For French academics in particular, and Europeans in general. He assumes that most, if not all, of them share his opinion, otherwise he would have shown some hesitation; he would have been cautious enough to wrap his words in the customary reserve.

As for Arab readers, it must have occurred to him that some of them might read or even translate him, which is exactly what happened. How did he imagine their reaction? It does not seem that he lent them much weight or thought it necessary to engage with them in discussion. The dialogue unfolding in his books mostly involves European readers. Clearly, he implicitly compares Arabic literature, which is boring, to European literature, which by contrast gives him pleasure and delight. And yet, he specialized in what is boring, and devoted his life to studying texts he did not appreciate and that did not move him. There is something tragic and pitiful in his predicament: he wasted his life on work for which he had no real desire or motivation.

Yet something saves him from despair and justifies his existence. There are Arabic books that he values and, in fact, greatly admires. If Arabic literature is boring, there are exceptions that prove the rule, or rather one exception: al-Jahiz. Pellat devoted most of his academic efforts to this writer, editing *Risalat al-tarbi' wa al-tadwir* [Epistle of the Square and the Circle] and translating *Kitab al-bukhala'* [*The Book of the Misers*], *Kitab al-taj* [Book of the Crown], and *Risalat al-qiyan* [Epistle of the Singing Maids]. He also published several studies of various aspects of al-Jahiz's life and thought. In short, his name is forever associated with al-Jahiz, just as Baudelaire's is associated with Edgar Allan Poe. Interestingly, he chose specifically an Arab writer who talked a great deal about boredom, who hardly wrote a book in which he does not address it. Al-Jahiz assumes that, as a rule, readers are quickly bored, that they are by nature susceptible to complaining about what they read, that at every moment they are tempted to put aside their book, and that, therefore, it is imperative to sustain their interest by various means, such as addressing them frequently, coaxing them, and diversifying the subjects presented to them. We could say that al-Jahiz invented the poetics of digression.

It is hard to say how al-Jahiz escaped the catastrophe that swept Arabic literature into the ocean of boredom, or the reason that led Charles Pellat to rescue him in particular from it. Nonetheless, there is one clue that might help us understand the motives of that French Arabist. In the aforementioned book, Pellat cites the German Orientalist Adam Mez, who compares al-Jahiz to Voltaire, but does not agree with him in this, believing that al-Jahiz is closer to the humanists, referring, no doubt, to writers like Erasmus, Rabelais, and Montaigne (Pellat 1953, ix). Whatever the case may be, several connections apparently exist between al-Jahiz and European literature. In that sense, he is, despite himself, European to some extent. Of course, it would not occur to Adam Mez to compare Voltaire to al-Jahiz, and Charles Pellat would not have said that Montaigne reminds him of al-Jahiz, which would be reasonable, at least in view of al-Jahiz's chronological precedence.

We move now to other Arab writers whom Charles Pellat discussed, this time in his book *Langue et littérature arabes* [Arabic Language and Literature, 1970]. He says that al-Tawhidi's *Mathalib al-wazirayn* [Defects of the Two Viziers] is "a satirical pamphlet some pages of which remind us of La Bruyère" (Pellat 1970, 139). As for al-Shidyaq's *Al-saq 'ala al-saq fi ma huwa al-Fariyaq* [Al-Fariyaq's Crossed Legs], it is "a critique of Near Eastern society influenced by Rabelais" (Pellat 1970, 204). How do we explain those references to French literature? It may be said that Charles Pellat is following a pedagogical method here, since he is addressing the general reader who is not familiar with Arabic literature and to whom it is necessary to introduce the unfamiliar through the familiar. That would certainly be a legitimate method, which can only be applauded.

However, it is a different matter when he says that Omar ibn Abi Rabi'a's popularity "is ever growing at the present time because of his resemblance to the great European love poets"

(1970, 85) and when he says that al-Ma'arri's *Risalat al-ghufran* [Epistle of Forgiveness] is "interesting for its relationship to the *Divine Comedy*" (1970, 119–20). Comparison here goes beyond the pedagogical goal and becomes a value judgment. *Risalat al-ghufran*, for example, is not important because of its own special characteristics, but for its resemblance to the *Divine Comedy*. No one would deny the resemblance between the two books, but what is distasteful is for that element to be what makes al-Ma'arri's book important—an odd reductionism based on deep contempt. Imagine, for a moment, that I am introducing Dante's book to Arab readers unfamiliar with it; would it be appropriate for me to say that it is interesting because of its similarity to *Risalat al-ghufran*? If I were to do so, I would be denying *The Divine Comedy*'s specificity and importance; its existence would be incidental, a being-for-Others, not for-itself, as philosophers would say. In this way, Charles Pellat does not inquire into al-Ma'arri's accomplishments but into his relationship to an Italian writer who came after him. And although al-Ma'arri becomes part of the family, he remains a poor cousin; without *The Divine Comedy*, he would not count.

Arabic literature is boring unless it bears a family resemblance to European literature. This family network is what rescues some Arabic books; outside of it, there is no hope of salvation. From this perspective, Arab authors fall into two categories: a small group of relatives and a great mass of orphans, beggars, and tramps. This view angers the Arab reader, without a doubt, especially that it is common to many Arabists, from Ernest Renan onward. But we must here return to the embarrassing question posed earlier: how do Arabs deal with their literature, and how do they see it? I am afraid that many of them take a position similar to that of Charles Pellat. Of course, I do not exclude myself; did I not introduce al-Hamadhani's *maqa-mat*, in the above-mentioned lecture, as though they belonged to the picaresque genre?

Needless to say, what I did was a species of comparative literature. Perhaps we could even say that every Arab reader is an experienced comparatist. Comparison is not restricted to specialists; rather, it embraces whoever approaches Arabic literature, ancient and modern. That is to say, the reader of an Arabic text soon connects it, directly or indirectly, to a European text. He is necessarily a comparatist, or we could say a translator.

To clarify, I shall turn to the Arab writer of old. Ibn Rushd (Averroës) did not learn Greek, and his knowledge of Aristotle and other philosophers was based on translations that were not all made directly from Greek. Did he ever feel the need to learn that language? Did he wish to read Aristotle in the original, without relying on translation? By the same token, Ibn Rushd was translated into Hebrew and Latin, then into other languages. Did he expect that? Did he write while conscious of the possibility that his works would some day be translated? We could pose the question differently: did Ibn Rushd hope to be translated? (We could also ask whether Aristotle had the same concern.)

Generally speaking, and aside from Ibn Rushd, did Arab authors take into account that their works might be translated into one or more foreign languages? How did they regard translation? It seems that they saw it as a one-way operation: from other languages (Persian, Greek, Syriac) into Arabic. As for the reverse, it likely did not occur to them, or at least did not worry them very much, perhaps because they assumed that those seeking knowledge and wisdom would have no choice but to master Arabic, which was exactly the case.

It is incontrovertible that the poetry of other peoples did not interest the Arabs. Moreover, they did not believe that their poetry should be translated, either, and we find this view expressed in al-Jahiz. In most cases, the question of translation is raised when two or more literatures jostle or compete. As it happened, Arabic literature had no competitor, or almost no opponent to speak of. For sure, the concept of literature was different in the classical than in the modern period, and we have to be very careful in this regard. Without getting into details, we could say that the question for the ancients was the intellectual production of different peoples, especially the Persians, the Greeks, and to a lesser extent the Indians. Arabic literature defined itself in the context of competition, separatism, and what was called *shu'ubiyyah*.[5] Yet the heated debates basically took place in Arabic. Arab men of letters addressed Arabic speakers, and the only translation they conceived of was exegesis, commentary, and annotation, that is, translation within the same language. Did Abu al-'Ala' al-Ma'arri, for instance, think about the translation of his works? To which language? For whom? For what purpose? How would he have reacted if, at one of his gatherings, someone raised the question of translating *Risalat al-ghufran* into Latin or Hebrew?

The ancients not only disdained and ignored translation, it seems that they unconsciously endeavored to make their works untranslatable. They developed formulations, modes of

---

5. *Shu'ubiyyah* (from *sha'b*, "a people or nation"), which may be rendered guardedly as "ethnonationalism," emerged during the early Abbasid period, when Persians were given prominent government positions that in the Umayyid period had been reserved for Arabs. The phenomenon challenged the heretofore-unquestioned political supremacy of Arabs within the Islamic world (translator's note).

expression, and styles difficult to translate. Perhaps one of the best examples of this is al-Hariri's *maqamat*, a book in which every sentence seems to say, "No one can possibly translate me!" It is as if al-Hariri did his utmost to protect his book from the tyranny of another tongue. Who would dare translate a text that remains the same when read from beginning to end and vice versa, or an epistle that reads one way from the beginning, and another way from the end? And who would venture to translate another in which dotted and undotted words alternate?[6] It has been said that al-Hariri aimed at demonstrating his linguistic dexterity, and he has been compared to an acrobat, but he certainly aimed at exhausting the hidden reserves of the Arabic language and realizing its full potential. As a result, his *maqamat* cannot be imagined in any language but Arabic and are impossible to translate. This is not only the case with al-Hariri's *maqamat*, but also with many ancient texts.

The ancients examined, realized, and used all the rhetorical possibilities, and they even went so far as to belittle and dismiss literature. They talked at length about its falsity and inutility, but they did so within its own framework and discursive norms. It never once occurred to them to look at it from the outside, through the lens of another literature. They never thought that the question of translating it would one day be raised. But that happened in the middle of the nineteenth century. Al-Shidyaq represents a turning point toward the shock of a bitter discovery: that Arabic literature is untranslatable, and that on the whole it matters only to Arabs.

6. The Arabic alphabet contains several letters that are differentiated from one another only by whether they carry diacritical dots and by the number of such dots (translator's note).

Since that time, the Arab writer, whether consciously on not, takes translation into account, that is, translation as comparison, evaluation, transformation of one literature into another. Every study of a modern Arab writer is, in effect, a comparative study. Who can read an Arab poet or novelist today without establishing a relationship between him and his European peers? We Arabs have invented a special way of reading: we read an Arabic text while thinking about the possibility of transferring it into a European language, with texts from French, English, or Italian literature in mind.[7] The fundamental change for us in the modern age is that the process of reading (and writing) is always attended with potential translation, the possibility of transfer into other literatures, something that never occurred to the ancients, who conceived of translation only within Arabic literature.

Translation has so dominated our horizon that it operates even when we read the ancients. We read *Hayy ibn Yaqdhan* and our minds wander to *Robinson Crusoe*; we read al-Mutanabbi and think of Nietzsche and the Will to Power; we read *Risalat al-ghufran* and willy-nilly *The Divine Comedy* appears before us; we read Abu al-'Ala' al-Ma'arri's *Luzum ma la yalzam* [The Necessity of What Is Unnecessary] in the light of Schopenhauer or Cioran; we read 'Abd al-Qahir al-Jurjani's *Dala'il al-i'jaz* [Signs of Inimitability] and suddenly we meet Saussure; we read Abu

---

7. An Egyptian professor has asserted to me that some Arab novelists write while thinking of their potential translators and endeavor to facilitate their task, for example by avoiding expressions and allusions which may not carry across into another language. The distant goal, in this case, is not writing a novel and publishing it in Arabic, but publishing it in translation. Thus in its composition, the novel looks to its transfer into English or French; it is written literally for those two languages.

Hamid al-Ghazali's *Al-Munqidh min al-dalal* [The Savior from Error] and Descartes comes to save us from confusion. Woe to the writers for whom we find no European counterparts: we simply turn away from them, leaving them in a dark, abandoned isthmus, a passage without mirrors to reflect their shadow or save them from loss and deathlike abandon. In short, we read the ancients with reference to European literature. Whenever an Arab writer approximates this literature, his marketability and popularity increase many times over, and the chances of his being translated improve.

2 ✦ The Translator

C an one possess two languages? Can one master them equally? We may not find the answer unless we ask another question: Can one possess any language? I remember hearing something, the source of which I have not yet been able to find, about one of the ancients who described his relationship to the Arabic language in this way: "I defeated her then she defeated me, then I defeated her and she defeated me again." His relationship with language is tense, and the war between them has its ups and downs, but language, this ferocious creature that refuses to be tamed, always has the last word. The battle always ends with her victory, leaving one no choice but to make truce and to surrender, however reluctantly.

If that is the predicament of the native speaker with his language, what would he do with two or more languages? How does he move from one to the other? How does he negotiate between them? How does he manage his affairs in perpetual translation? I shall approach this topic with reference to al-Jahiz [A.D. 776–869], a writer of whose knowledge of another language besides Arabic we cannot be sure, although there are indications in his work that he knew Persian.

Let us begin with what he says in *Al-Bayan wa al-tabyyin* [Rhetoric and Exposition] about Abu-Ali al-Uswari, who lectured in one mosque "for thirty-six years. He began with the exegesis of the sura of the Cow and did not finish the Qur'an until he died. Since he knew the biographies and the canonical interpretations, he could spend several weeks on the exegesis of one verse" (n.d., 1: 367). Explaining the Qur'an is a very long process that ends only with the life of the interpreter. Which language did al-Uswari use in his interpretation? Arabic, of course, and it seems that his audience was composed mainly of Arabs and of non-Arabs who had acquired Arabic. But how was the Book of God explained to those who did not know the language in which it was revealed?

The question would not have occurred to me if that passage were not adjacent to another one in which al-Jahiz describes another interpreter called Musa ibn Sayyar al-Uswari: "He was one of the wonders of the world. He was as eloquent in Persian as he was in Arabic. At his famous gatherings, he would sit with Arabs to his right and Persians to his left. He would recite a verse from the Book of God, explain it in Arabic to the Arabs, then turn toward the Persians and explain it to them in Persian. It was not known in which language he excelled" (1: 367).

Arabs on one side, Persians on the other. There is no mingling or assimilation between the two groups, each of which remains within its circumscribed place. A fortified barrier separates the two, namely the difference in tongue. Only the preacher knows the two languages, so that it is "not known in which language he excelled," for he explains the Book of God in Arabic, then in Persian, with equal ease. If we consider interpretation to be translation within a particular language, then he undertakes two translations, into Arabic then into Persian (notice that he begins with Arabic, which is significant). And each time he turns to one side, to his right when addressing Arabs and to his left when addressing Persians. To speak is to turn, with the attendant associations of the two directions, two sides, two locations. Is it a coincidence that Arabs sit to his right and Persians to his left? Can we imagine the reverse? If Arabs sat to his left and Persians to his right, Arabic would have become secondary to Persian, which would have never occurred to Musa ibn Sayyar or to al-Jahiz. How could that be when the original text being interpreted was revealed in Arabic?

What we learn from this scene is that to speak a language necessitates turning to one side. Language is tied to a location on the map or to a given space. To speak this or that language is to be on the right or on the left. As for the bilingual, he is in constant movement, always turning, and since he looks in two directions, he is two-faced.

Expressing his admiration and amazement at this predicament, al-Jahiz says, "When two languages meet on one tongue, each of them injures her companion [that is, the other language], except on the aforementioned tongue of Musa ibn Sayyar al-Uswari" (1: 367). Although al-Jahiz's categorical assertion that no one can ever master two languages gives us cause for pessimism, we may also find comfort in it, or resignation at the inevitable, for the failure to possess two languages is not the result of slackness or negligence but because human beings, whatever their skills, are incapable of doing so. There is, then, a general rule, that is, the total impossibility of the free use of two languages by reason of their antagonism. This is what al-Jahiz's use of the word *daym* ["harm," "injustice," "injury"] indicates: "one of them injures [or harms] her companion." It is a matter of mutual injustice and belittlement. There are no oppressive and oppressed languages; when they "meet on one tongue," each is simultaneously an aggressor and a victim. Their relationship is not built on peaceful coexistence but, to the contrary, on tugging, opposition, and quarrel. Al-Jahiz subtly implies that they are like co-wives [*darratayn*]; according to Ibn Mandhur, co-wives "are called *darratayn* because each of them harms her companion," and because "co-wives [*dara'ir*] do not agree."[1]

That rule has only one exception, Musa ibn Sayyar, who managed to join Arabic and Persian on his tongue and to treat them justly, so that they did not conflict with one another. (By association, the name of this preacher recalls the prophet Moses and his tense relationship with language: "untie my tongue so that they may understand my words" (Qur'an 20:28–29). However, this exception raises for us a subtle problem that may have escaped al-Jahiz: who could possibly determined whether Musa ibn Sayyar mastered Arabic and Persian completely and equally? Al-Jahiz, of course. Yet he does not claim that he knows Persian, or that he knows it as well as he knows Arabic. He has, therefore, no authority to judge the case. For his opinion to be valid, he must then rely on authorities who know both languages perfectly and who could certify that Musa ibn Sayyar has completely mastered both languages. But where can such authorities be found? If we assume they exist, al-Jahiz's assertion about the impossibility of complete bilingualism would be refuted, and Musa ibn Sayyar would no longer be an exception. Unless we suppose that some of those hypothetical judges represent one language, and some the other, so that they would assess him separately: Arabs on one side, Persians on the other.

---

1. *Darrah* (dual *darratayn*, plural *dara'ir*) is from the root verb *darra*, meaning "to harm." The Qur'anic command to treat co-wives justly and with absolute equality amounts, according to some interpretations, to a de facto prohibition on polygamy: "If you fear that you cannot be equitable [to them], then marry only one" (Qur'an 4:3); "You will never be able to treat your wives with equal fairness, however much you may desire to do so" (4:129). Al-Jahiz's view of bilingualism is rhetorically framed by the Qur'anic discourse on polygamy (translator's note).

To take al-Jahiz's opinion seriously, we would have to ask about his view of translation. Does he not suggest that it is impossible to all but Musa ibn Sayyar? He implies that this interpreter of the Qur'an is the ideal translator, next to whom other translators are deficient by degrees, according to the level of their knowledge of the two languages. The rule stated in *Al-bayan wa al-tabyyin* is that translation is impossible, that any translation is inevitably deficient.

That is also exactly the conclusion he reaches in *Kitab al-hayawan* when he raises an issue pertaining, this time, not to the interpretation of the Qur'an in Arabic and Persian, but to the translation of philosophical books from Greek into Arabic. Al-Jahiz says of the translator, "Whenever we also find him speaking two languages, we know that he has mistreated both of them, for each one of the two languages pulls at the other, takes from it, and opposes it" (1996, 1: 76). To put this passage (which does not much differ from what came in *Al-Bayan wa al-tabyyin*) in its general context, we must point out that in the introduction to *Kitab al-hayawan*, al-Jahiz addresses a special type of reader, one who antagonizes him and belittles his books. Who is this obstinate opponent who is not content to belittle al-Jahiz's books but goes so far in his disdain as to demean all books? "Then I saw that you were not content to attack each one of my books, but went on to dismiss the writing of all manner of books. I used to wonder at your finding fault with some books without reading them, until you found fault with all books, also without reading them; then you exceeded that by resorting to slander; then you exceeded that, too, by declaring war and denouncing writers" (38). Why this scorn for books? What is behind it?

In the roughly one-hundred-page introduction to *Kitab al-hayawan*, al-Jahiz raises many different issues, but despite his numerous digressions, we could say that his concerns revolve around the question of the book, or of writing. If we trace this thread, it becomes clear that there are those who find fault with books and those who praise them. Within this conflict between two opposing tendencies, al-Jahiz takes up the question of translation, specifically the translation of poetry and philosophy.

With regard to Greek philosophy, he gives two reasons for the failure or deficiency of translation. "The translator never renders what the wise man says in the specificity of its meaning and its true doctrine. How could he convey the meaning accurately and truthfully unless his knowledge of it and the words used to express it and their nuances equal those of the author? Did Ibn al-Bitriq, God bless his soul, or Ibn Na'imah, Ibn Qurrah, Ibn Fihriz, Ibn Wahili, and Ibn al-Muqaffa' ever equal Aristotle? Was Khalid ever like Plato?" (1996, 75–76). Translation is deficient because the translator's knowledge is not as deep as the philosopher's. No matter how broad his knowledge or how familiar he is with the subject matter of the book he is translating, the translator remains incapable of equaling the author.

Then there is a second obstacle that al-Jahiz points out: "The degree of the translator's clarity of expression must equal the degree of his knowledge of the subject, and he must be the most knowledgeable of all people of the source language and the target language, so that he masters them equally. Whenever we also find him speaking two languages, we know that he has mistreated both of them, since each of the two pulls at the other, takes from it, and opposes it. How could his mastery of both of them together ever equal his mastery of only one?" (1996, 76).

In this text, al-Jahiz does not make exception for anyone with regard to the impossibility of translation, unlike in *Al-Bayan wa al-tabyyin*, where he elevates Musa ibn Sayyar, the interpreter of the Qur'an, above other translators and considers him one of the wonders of the world. The translation of philosophy is always characterized by deficiency and failure. He does not try to hide his disdain for those who translated from Greek; indeed, he expresses his contempt for them: "When did Khalid ever equal Plato?"[2] Once again, we cannot but express our amazement at this comparison. How did al-Jahiz determine that Khalid is lesser than Plato? In order to issue a judgment like that, you have to have studied the works of both of them, and you have to know Arabic and Greek. Al-Jahiz does not claim that, but does he not imply that there is someone who is capable of such an assessment and who can demonstrate Plato's superiority to Khalid, somebody who could discern the errors and lapses of translators, and who would therefore seek to correct them? Does the deficiency of translators negate the effort to remedy that deficiency and to bring the translation and the original within great proximity to one another?

Before delving into the subject of the translation of philosophy, al-Jahiz discusses the translation of poetry. He is of the opinion that "poetry cannot, and should not, be translated. When translated, its rhyme is disrupted, its meter ruined, its beauty lost, and its wonder fades" (1996, 1: 75).

It is impossible to translate poetry because of a special characteristic, meter, which is destroyed when poetry is transferred into a different idiom. Noticeably, al-Jahiz does not accuse translators of incompetence, and does not blame their imperfect

---

2. About this Khalid al-Jahiz says, "Khalid ibn Yazid ibn Mu'awiya was an orator and a poet, eloquent and erudite, with good judgment and literary taste. He was the first to translate books of astronomy, medicine, and chemistry" (al-Jahiz n.d., 1: 328).

knowledge of the two languages for their failure to translate poetry, the way he blames the translators of philosophy. Even if we were to postulate the existence of a perfect translator, one who knows both languages better than anyone else, the problem would remain with regard to poetry. The reason for the difficulty in translating Greek philosophy is the translators' deficient knowledge of philosophy and their lack of equal mastery of Arabic and Greek. As for the impossibility of translating poetry, al-Jahiz does not see it as the result of translators' incompetence, but of the impossibility of translating poetry in the first place. However skillful the translator, poetry refuses translation, and if it is transferred from its original language into another one, it loses its value and becomes a distorted, disfigured text.

We may agree with al-Jahiz and welcome his opinion on the impossibility of translating poetry. We may share his view that poetry flourishes within a specific language, and withers and dies when transplanted into another. However, we are amazed and feel the utmost reserve when we read the sentence immediately preceding the above-quoted passage: "The gift of poetry is restricted to the Arabs and to those who speak their language." This is a notorious statement, often quoted and commented on by scholars, who have explicitly and implicitly shown their amazement at it.

How could that be? How did al-Jahiz come to hold such a belief? Why does he claim that poetry is restricted to Arabs? It is true that he does not exclude non-Arabs entirely from poetry, but on the condition that they learn the language of the Arabs and compose poetry in it. Perhaps he had in mind poets of Persian origin who excelled in Arabic poetry, such as Bashshar ibn Burd and Abu Nuwas. From this perspective, poetry is not so much tied to Arabs as a race or ethnicity as it is to the Arabic language. But this does not relieve our confusion and unease. Did al-Jahiz not know that poetry is found in all languages? Yes, indeed, for in *Al-Bayan wa al-tabyyin* (as well as in *Kitab al-hayawan*), he mentions Disymus [*sic*],[3] who "was one of the deluded among the Greeks. Someone asked him, 'Why does Disymus teach others poetry but cannot compose it himself?' He replied, 'He is like the whetstone that sharpens but does not cut'" (n.d., 2: 226; 1996, 1: 290).

We may say that al-Jahiz's statement belongs in the context of competition between nations, which was one aspect of the empire of Islam at the time, and part of long, complicated disputes among several cultures. Al-Jahiz took part in that dispute, authoring several books including *Kitab al-ʿArab wa al-mawali* [The Book of Arabs and Subject Peoples] and *Kitab al-ʿArab wa al-ʿAjam* [The Book of Arabs and non-Arabs]. If we take this tense atmosphere into account, we could feign stupidity and understand why al-Jahiz would be so rash as to declare poetry one of the special characteristics of the Arabs and an art exclusive to them. Yet this does not explain or make palatable the stark contradiction.

More reason for astonishment is that al-Jahiz, having asserted that poetry is restricted to Arabs, adds the following: "Indian books have been transferred, Greek wisdom has been translated, and Persian literature has been adapted into Arabic. Some of those books increased in beauty, and some lost none of their own" (1996, 1: 75). Translations of the wisdom of other

3. The reference is likely to Isocrates, not Didymus (of which Disimus is probably a corruption). The report appears in *Lives of the Ten Orators*, attributed to Plutarch (http://classicpersuasion.org/pw/plu10or/pluisoc .htm, July 19, 2006) (translator's note).

nations, including the Greeks, retain the value of the original, losing nothing, and may indeed be better than the original! This contradicts the earlier statements about the impossibility of translating Greek philosophy. How could this other contradiction escape al-Jahiz? How could he say in one paragraph that translation distorts philosophy, and in a nearby paragraph that translation increases its beauty?

It is time to ask ourselves a question that may seem contrived, but it would help us emerge from this confusion: did al-Jahiz in fact say that poetry is a gift confined to Arabs? This judgment is without a doubt stated verbatim in *Kitab al-hayawan*, but is it justifiable to attribute it to al-Jahiz?

In returning to the text, and to the paragraph concerning the incompetence of the translator of philosophy and his failure to render Greek thought, it became clear, to my surprise, that it is preceded by the following phrase, "Some of those who defend and advocate for poetry have said." The source of the statement on the impossibility of translating philosophy is not al-Jahiz, but some other unnamed person. The same goes for the paragraph in which we read that poetry is a gift restricted to Arabs; it does not necessarily express al-Jahiz's opinion, since it is preceded by "he said." He refers to someone else's opinion, and it would be risky to attribute it to al-Jahiz without scrutiny.

Moreover, as soon as we begin rereading the pages surrounding the two passages, it becomes clear to us that a sort of (Platonic) dialogue between two people or two antagonists is taking place. This is evidenced by the fact that several of the surrounding paragraphs begin with "he said," "they said," "the other one said."

Al-Jahiz does not speak in his own voice but rather attributes speech to others, which is a favorite and frequently used technique of his, not only in *Kitab al-hayawan* but in all his books and letters. This requires us to be careful not to jump too soon to the conclusion that he necessarily accepts the opinions he presents, just as when reading a novel, we do not judge that what the characters say necessarily reflects the author's beliefs.

There is, then, in *Kitab al-hayawan*, a defender of poetry who claims that translations of Greek philosophy are deficient and who does not hide his contempt for translators, and another who claims that the gift of poetry is confined to Arabs and that poetry cannot be translated. Are these two persons or one? We may be inclined to believe that it is one person, that the one who defends poetry (Arabic poetry, of course) and asserts that nobody can master two languages may be the same one who declares that poetry is restricted to Arabs. He may be an Arab himself, or at least a champion and defender of Arabs. And indeed to whom but an Arab, in the context of competition between nations, would it occur to restrict poetry to the Arabs and those who speak Arabic?

This is what I used to think, until it became clear to me that the statement about poetry being restricted to Arabs is not cited in the context of praise, but as a reservation and a caution. The speaker does not consider poetry to be an advantage for the Arabs, something for them to be proud of among other nations. For what does he mean when he adds that poetry cannot and should not be translated? He means that non-Arabs cannot benefit from it, that its profit is restricted to the Arabs and those who speak their language. So in that sense, he is belittling poetry and arguing against it.

Let us examine the context of this passage and the manner of its presentation. We have already pointed out that the introduction to *Kitab al-hayawan* treats the subject of writing and books. The reader postulated and addressed by al-Jahiz denounces books. Al-Jahiz responds to him by extolling them and explaining their merit at length. Among other things, he says in defense of the book, "What excellent treasure, what excellent company, what excellent entertainment, what excellent employment, what an excellent friend for the hour of solitude" (1996, 38).

In the course of this defense comes the following passage, preceded by "he said": "Each nation relies, for the preservation of its glory and the enshrinement of its virtues, on some genre or form. Pre-Islamic Arabs contrived to achieve immortality though poetry and patterned speech; that was their divan. . . . Non-Arabs recorded their achievements in architecture. . . . such as Ardashir who erected Bayda' Istakhr and Bayda' al-Mada'in, as well as towns, cities, castles, arched bridges, dams, and sarcophagi" (72).

After that, we find, once again, "he said": "The Arabs wished to emulate non-Arabs in architecture, while having poetry all to themselves, so they built Ghumdan, the ka'ba of Nijran, and the palaces of Marid, Ma'rib, Sha'ub, and al-Ablaq al-Fard . . . among other buildings" (72).

Once again, "he said" appears: "For that reason, the Persians did not permit the construction of noble buildings, just as they do not allow noble names, except for notable families, and the same goes for their sarcophagi, public baths, green domes, wall-mounted balconies, vaulted corridors, and the like" (72).

Immediately after that, we read this: "some of those present said." It is a very strange sentence because the context does not prepare for it. Who was present, where, when, with whom, how, why? We are completely in the dark. It seems that there was a gathering of several people of different backgrounds, tastes, and inclinations, and that they were engaged in comparing the merits and demerits of different nations. However, there is no mention of such a gathering in *Kitab al-hayawan*. If you were to say, "some of those present said," that would necessarily mean that you have talked about those present and described their gathering, something that never occurs in the book. We would be justified in wondering whether the text has been tampered with, and if whatever was said about that gathering had been omitted. Otherwise, how do we explain the clause, "some of those present said"?

Whatever the case may be, let us read what this man says: "The books of wise and learned men . . . are more permanent, more distinguished, and more profitable, because wisdom is a better legacy to those who use it, and a better reputation to those who seek to be well remembered" (73). He is an advocate of books, no doubt. After someone said that Arabs contrived to immortalize themselves through poetry and non-Arabs though architecture, and after someone (the same person?) said that Arabs combined the two virtues in that they constructed monuments like non-Arabs and were peerless in poetry, this fellow says that books are more permanent and more distinguished. To further support his claim, he adds: "Books, therefore, have precedence over stones and mud-brick walls, since kings tend to erase the traces of those who came before them and to kill the memory of their enemies" (73).

After this comparison of books to buildings, he goes on to say, "As for poetry, it is of recent origin and young age. The first to follow its path were Imru'ul-Qays ibn Hujr and Muhalhil ibn Rabi'ah. The books of Aristotle, his teacher Plato, Ptolemy,

Democritus, and others preceded poetry by many long ages. . . . If we investigate poetry, we find that it began one hundred and fifty, or at most two hundred, years before Islam" (74).

Why does he weigh poetry against philosophy? What does he mean by emphasizing that Arabic poetry was born recently, while Greek philosophy is age-old? There is no question that he posits that philosophy is not only greater in age than poetry, but also in value, as though temporal precedence gives philosophy worth, advantage, and priority, while the belatedness of poetry is a sign of its childishness, naïveté, and immaturity. Philosophy is like an experienced and sagacious old man, whereas poetry is like a foolish and frivolous boy whose words are not to be taken seriously. Poetry came late and without warning. One day, it was suddenly born with Muhalhil and Imru'ul-Qays, who had no predecessors. Poetry was at most two centuries old by the time of Islam (that is, four centuries old in al-Jahiz's time), no more. And if the origin of poetry is precisely known, the origin of philosophy is not; it is quasi-eternal, sprung from the depths of a distant past.

Finally, this person arrives at the puzzling point, "The gift of poetry is restricted to the Arabs and to those who speak their language. Poetry cannot and should not be translated."

These views, which are usually ascribed to al-Jahiz, now take on another dimension, and their import changes, since they belong to one of the advocates of Greek philosophy. He does not mean that only Arabs are capable of composing poetry, but that poetry benefits no one but its own people, that other nations have nothing to gain from it, unlike the books of non-Arabs: "If the wisdom of the Arabs were to be translated, its miracle, which is meter, would be undone. Even if it is translated, there would not be found in it anything that non-Arabs had not said in their books, which enhance their lives, their intelligence, and their government. Those books were transferred from nation to nation, from century to century, from language to language, until they reached us. We were the last to inherit and study them. It is true, therefore, that books are more eloquent records of glorious deeds than monuments or poetry" (75).

When he reaches this conclusion, his opponent, who champions poetry, emerges to disparage and belittle the translation of philosophy on the grounds that the translator, as mentioned earlier, does not possess knowledge equal to that of the author, and because mastering two languages is impossible. He then goes on to talk about the corruption of books due to copiers' errors and wonders, "How could such books be more beneficial to their people than rhymed poetry?" (79). (Interestingly, this sentence is preceded by "they said.")

However, while acknowledging the shortcomings of translation and the corruption resulting from copiers' errors, the advocate of Greek philosophy does not think that they decrease the value and benefit of books: "Is it not clear that something the value of which endures despite such great damage, and the power of which withstands such corruption, deserves to be valued over architecture, and preferred to a poetry that breaks down when translated, and whose benefit is restricted to its people?" (79–80). The universality of philosophy contrasts with the particularity of poetry; and since philosophy is not tied to a specific language, it benefits all people, whereas poetry benefits only Arabs.

We conclude from this dialogue that there is a fundamental opposition between philosophy and poetry: philosophy can be translated to the benefit of all people, while poetry benefits only Arabs. Upon further scrutiny, it becomes clear that there are several levels to this comparison. The contrast between poetry and philosophy parallels the contrast between the oral and the written, what is new (poetry) and what is ancient (philosophy), and the Arabs and non-Arabs, particularly the Greeks.

Those contrasts can be divided into two categories: orality and writing. On the one hand, we have the Arabic language, poetry, untranslatability, orality, newness, Arab origin, and particularity; on the other hand, we have the Greek language, prose, philosophy, translatability, writing, old age, non-Arab origin, and universality. In the context of this general opposition, and in a dialogue or almost in a dialogue between two or more people, the question of translation is raised.

It remains for us to ask what al-Jahiz's position is in this conversation. To which camp does he belong? Let us recall his response to the one who denounces books, starting with al-Jahiz's own. That suggests that he is in the writing camp, opposite those in the orality camp. Yet things are not so simple, for al-Jahiz as usual disappears behind characters to whom he ascribes opinions, within a context of disputation and controversy. He is present and absent, distributing opinions to the representatives of this or that position, and withholding his own viewpoint. He does not arbitrate or offer the final word. Even when he speaks in the first person, in his own name, his opinion takes no precedence over others' because it also aligns with the opposite views. He is a writer who for the most part appears to be without location.[4]

By the same token, one point deserves full scrutiny, but I will only mention it here: al-Jahiz is unable to compose a book!

---

4. In commenting on the expression "more lost than a snake," he says, "a snake has no fixed residence; wherever it finds a hole, it enters it" (1996, 4: 169).

This judgment may appear silly and counterfactual. Does he not have hundreds of works to his name? Yet he did not regard them as books, in the full sense of the word, and he often apologizes for his inability to compose a book, with what that requires of structuring, division into chapters, development of an argument, and organization. There is plenty of evidence to support that, including his rapid and unexpected shifts of topics and direction, his mixing of the serious and the humorous, and his constant address to the reader. In talking about his books, he sometimes gives the impression that he considers his digressions to be a defect, for he justifies them by his desire not to bore the reader. Yet does that not suggest that he could not completely abandon "orality," "poetry," and reporting conversations that take place at gatherings and banquets, and that are governed only by the immediate desires of those present?

In the final analysis, al-Jahiz belongs to the two above-mentioned camps, which is what he himself asserts in the introduction to *Kitab al-hayawan* when he says, "In this book, the desires of nations are seen as similar and Arabs and non-Arabs are treated equally; for while it is Arab-Bedouin, and Islamic of the orthodox community, it has taken part in philosophy" (1996, 1: 11). He addresses two kinds of readers (that is, his book is two books in one), and consequently, like Musa ibn Sayyar al-Uswari, he turns to both sides, to the right and to the left.

3 ✦ Illusion

The history of Averroism is, properly speaking, nothing
but the history of an enormous misinterpretation.

—Ernest Renan

I f Petrarch hated Arabs and everything related to them, so
much so that when taken ill he refused medications bearing Arabic names (Renan 1997, 234–35), his contemporary
Dante, by contrast, was partial to them, as evidenced by his
great admiration for Ibn Rushd [Averroes, A.D. 1126–98]. Had
he not been constrained by some considerations, he would have
admitted him to Paradise. Still, he did not throw him in Hell,
but gave him a quiet place in Limbo next to Plato and Aristotle.
It may have even pained Dante that the philosopher of Cordova
could not be placed in Paradise, so he skillfully redressed the
situation by reserving a distinguished place there for Siger of
Brabant, a Latin philosopher who championed Averroism and
suffered greatly because of his allegiance to it.

Dante said that Ibn Rushd "made the great commentary"
[*Inferno* 4.144], meaning the commentary on Aristotle's *Metaphys-
ics.* Yet there is another, no less famous commentary by Ibn Rushd
on the *Poetics,* which may be regarded, from a certain perspective,
as infamous. Ibn Rushd, who tried to be completely faithful to
Aristotle, betrayed him this time and distorted his ideas—inad-
vertently, of course, and without once suspecting it. Overall, it is

an unreadable commentary, which does not enrich anyone's understanding of the *Poetics*. If Aristotle's book were lost, we would not be able to imagine its subject or content from reading Ibn Rushd. Moreover, to understand the latter, we have to return to Aristotle, an irony that many readers must have discerned: it is not Ibn Rushd who explains Aristotle, but the other way around!

Ibn Rushd's summary of the *Poetics* seems to us cryptic and confusing, but then, from his viewpoint, the *Poetics* was obscure and ambiguous. Despite his well-known erudition and the diversity of his interests, the greatest medieval philosopher did not understand this book. The reason for that is that he was interpreting a discussion of Greek literature, of which he had no knowledge. That being the case, misunderstanding was inevitable.

He understood, at least, that the *Poetics*, as it reached him, was incomplete. He wrote, "This book was not completely translated and . . . there are still many other sorts of subdivisions of their poems that remain to be discussed. And in the introduction to his book he had promised to speak about all these things. With respect to the common statements, the discussion of the art of satire is missing" (Ibn Rushd 1986, 141). The missing part of the book was not the fault of the Arab translator, for Matta ibn Yunus, on whom Ibn Rushd probably relied, found himself faced with an amputated book, without the section devoted to comedy (or satire, as Ibn Rushd understood it).[1] The part in which Aristotle discusses comedy had been lost before Matta ibn Yunus translated the book.[2]

1. As we know, Matta ibn Yunus translated "tragedy" as "panegyric" and "comedy" as "satire."

2. See Umberto Eco's use of this lost part of *Poetics* in his novel *The Name of the Rose*.

If Ibn Rushd's commentary does not help us at all in understanding the *Poetics*, it helps us a great deal in understanding the philosopher of Cordova and his intellectual horizon. Ibn Rushd knew only Arabic poetry. He was familiar with its various genres—panegyric, satire, elegy, love poetry—and its forms—ode, muwashshah, zajal. Other than poetry, he alludes to proverbs and stories, especially those in *Kalila wa Dimna*, as well as to Islamic legal texts, the sunna, the story of Abraham and that of "Joseph, God's blessing upon him, and his brothers as well as other short stories that are called exhortations" (Ibn Rushd 1986, 92). All of that knowledge did not help him understand Aristotle, for what is beyond his and his contemporaries' horizon is the theater. As we know, tragedy and comedy had no equivalent in Arabic before the nineteenth century. Thus, Ibn Rushd, who knew nothing of the theater, undertook to interpret a book specifically about that. He wrote about genres that were alien to him, thinking that tragedy was panegyric and that comedy was satire. He had to look ahead of him, not behind him, yet he looked behind him and lost Eurydice. But he did not mind the loss, for he had never seen her before or fallen in love with her.

Some believe that misunderstanding and misinterpretation could be fruitful, yielding new connections and original, creative readings. Yet this could not possibly be the case with the sort of misunderstanding we are talking about, which was sterile, neither opening new horizons nor producing anything more than a farce—the ridiculous and highly embarrassing story of a great philosopher who did not grasp the meaning of tragedy and comedy. Today, we understand the *Poetics*, or imagine that we do; at least we know what tragedy and comedy are, what theatrical performance is. As for Ibn Rushd, he did not know that and had no one around to explain his error to him.

For some, this story is a source of bitterness and repressed anger felt over lost opportunity. The meeting of Arabic and Greek literatures was possible but did not happen. How do we explain that? How do we explain the Arabs' lack of interest in Greek literature, despite their strong and abiding interest in Greek philosophy? Why did they translate Plato and Aristotle, but not Homer and Sophocles?

Much has been written on this topic. For example, it has been said that Arabs fell victims to hubris, that they thought so highly of their poetry that they took no interest in the poetry of others. Why translate foreign poetry that is necessarily inferior to Arabic poetry? This explanation is unconvincing: it is true that Arabs revered their poetry, but how could they deem worthless the Greek poetic genres, of which they knew nothing? It may be said that their weakness and error lay precisely in their lack of interest, which led to grave negligence. Arabs would be guilty, in this case, of ignorance and indifference. They ought to have taken an interest in Greek literature, but unfortunately they did not; theater was within their reach and they stupidly turned away from it.

However, upon scrutiny it becomes clear that the matter had nothing to do with hubris or indifference, and that there was another reason why they contented themselves with their own poetry and stayed away from the Greek, a reason that has to do with translation.

Let us return to al-Jahiz's comparison, in *Kitab al-hayawan*, between Greek philosophy and Arabic poetry. We concluded from it that philosophy is translatable while poetry is not. Plato and Aristotle could be translated without any significant loss, whereas translated poetry (poetry being above all metrical composition) can only be poor and revolting. It is useless and silly to read a translated poem; whatever its beauty, the poem becomes a threadbare tissue of inanities when transposed into another language.

If Arabic poetry is untranslatable and can only be read or recited in its original language, its benefit is restricted to Arabs and those who know their language, while others would not appreciate or benefit from it. Although al-Jahiz does not say so explicitly, he surely believed that what was true of Arabic poetry was also true of other poetries, whatever their language. The defining characteristic of poetry is its untranslatability. Consequently, Greek poetry can only be read in Greek. Each poetry is tied to a specific language in which it can be appreciated; it is forever confined to its original language. This is not so with philosophy, which can be received beyond its original language. While it is necessary to know Arabic to read Imru'ul-Qays and al-Nabigha, it is not necessary to know Greek to read Plato and Aristotle.

It is likely that Ibn Rushd adopted this point of view. At any rate, he read Greek philosophers in Arabic, and as far as I know he did not regret that he did not know Greek, to which philosophy was not necessarily tied, according to al-Jahiz. By the same token Ibn Rushd did not show any interest in reading Greek poetry, which cannot be read in any other language.[3]

Nevertheless, he was anxious vis-à-vis this unknown poetry while commenting on the *Poetics*. He was conscious of the book's resistance to him, and at each step he confronted a difficult

---

3. It would be helpful to know what Aristotle thought of translating philosophy and poetry. It seems that he was not preoccupied with the poetry of other nations; if I am not mistaken, his *Poetics* is concerned only with Greek poetry.

obstacle. While he was grossly mistaken from beginning to end, he felt that Aristotle's text interrogated him and challenged him to crack its code. Yet he was incapable of doing so because of his unfamiliarity with Greek poetry, which, like any poetry—to emphasize once more—could only be read in its original language. Time after time, he would be vexed and annoyed, then he would explain away the difficulty by saying that such matters relate to their poetry and concern them alone.

As we know, Greek literature never came within the orbit of his interests, meaning that it was not the reason for his attempt to summarize the *Poetics*. He announces that much in the opening lines: "The purpose of this discussion is to comment upon those universal rules in Aristotle's *Poetics* that are common to all or most nations, for much of its contents are ... rules particularly characteristic of their poems" (Ibn Rushd 1986, 59). Yet he only found specifics. Thus he says, for example, without noticing the contradiction, "These are the matters in this chapter that are common to all or most nations. All or most of the rest of what he mentions is particular to their poems and their customs with respect to them" 1986, 70). He searches for the universal, but only finds the particular, what is unique to the Greeks.

He does not much care for the uniqueness of Greek poetry or, for that matter, the uniqueness of Arabic poetry. Nevertheless, he has no choice but to become engrossed in particulars, and even to compare the two poetries. He says of Greek poetry, "Their customs in it are either attributes found in the speech of the Arabs or [only] in other languages" (Ibn Rushd 1986, 59).[4] He favors the second possibility, suggesting that Arabs departed

4. Butterworth's translation of this passage has been modified (translator's note).

from what was common to other nations, which is what he suggests in this odd passage: "All of that is particular to them, and
no example of it is to be found among us either because what
he mentioned is not common to most nations or because with
respect to these things something apart from what is natural
occurred to the Arabs—and this is more likely. After all, he
[would] not [have] set down in this book of his what is peculiar
to them but what is common to natural nations" (1986, 136).

He would not have set down what is peculiar to them! At the
same time, he points out that all or most of the *Poetics* concerns
what is specific to them. His position is marked by confusion
and hesitation, yet he settles the matter finally by assuming that
Arabic poetry departs from the norm. He is more prepared to
regard Arabic poetics as the exception than to admit that Aristotle spoke only of the conventions of Greek poetry. Thus he
reaches the inevitable conclusion that what Aristotle proposes
is common to all nations, and that it is only Arabs who deviate
from it. Arabic poetry, which is all that Ibn Rushd knows, is
beyond the norm. Something happened to the Arabs to prevent
them from writing poetry the way others did. They lost their
way and deviated from the path of "natural nations."[5]

I feel embarrassed as I write these lines, for despite myself, I
speak of Ibn Rushd with a certain amount of condescension. I
am embarrassed because I know what he did not! Besides, who
would be immune from error when expounding on the errors of
his predecessors? Therefore, I doubt myself and ask, what gross
error could I have committed while speaking of Ibn Rushd's
error? Perhaps Borges entertained the same doubt when he
ended his short story "Averroës' Search" by saying,

---

5. I do not know exactly what Ibn Rushd means by this obscure phrase.

I recalled Averroës, who, bounded within the circle of Islam, could never know the meaning of the words *tragedy* and *comedy*. I told his story; as I went on, I felt what that god mentioned by Burton must have felt—the god who set himself the task of creating a bull but turned out a buffalo. I felt that the work mocked me, foiled me, thwarted me. I felt that Averroës, trying to imagine what a play is without ever having suspected what theater is, was no more absurd than I, trying to imagine Averroës yet with no more material than a few snatches from Renan, Lane, and Asín Palacio.[6] (Borges 1998, 241)

6. See my article on this story, "Borges et Averroès." [Translator's note: Charles Butterworth has this to say in the introduction to his translation of Ibn Rushd: "For too long non-Arabic readers have been dependent on Hermannus Alemannus' Latin translation of Averroes's *Middle Commentary on Aristotle's Poetics* or on O. B. Hardinson's English translation of the Latin. They incorrectly render Averroes' various arguments and make his beautiful citations read like doggerel. Moreover, they provide inaccurate and incomplete information about the sources of those citations and thereby portray Averroes' text as a curious compilation of relics from some exotic but not very learned horde. Consequently, Ernest Renan's contemptuous dismissal of Averroes for his ignorance of Greek poetry and Luis Borgès' facetious tale of Averroes' futile efforts to understand what Aristotle meant by tragedy and comedy remain virtually uncontested. Not even the publication of the Arabic original of Averroes' commentary on four separate occasions during the last 115 years has remedied this deplorable situation" (1986, ix).]

4 ✦ Between Movement and Stillness

Happy is he who, like Odysseus, after a beautiful journey,
Or he who captured the Golden Fleece,
Returned full of experience and wisdom,
To live out his life among his kin.

—Du Bellay

When he left the Maldives on his way to China, Ibn Battuta [A.D. 1304–68] came upon a small island "in which there was but one house, occupied by a weaver. He had a wife and family, a few coco-palms and a small boat, with which he used to fish. . . . And I swear I envied that man, and wished that the island had been mine, that I might have made it my retreat until the inevitable hour should befall me" (Ibn Battuta 1958–2000, 4: 845).

This weaver is a poor man living almost in a state of nature on an isolated island, surviving on the fruit of the few trees and the catch of the sea, and by virtue of his profession, he makes his own clothes. He enjoys a quiet life with his wife and children, content with his lot, dependent on no one, and with no care in the world. It is an image of happiness and tranquility, hence Ibn Battuta's envious wish that he were in a similar situation. In fact, this wish would not have been difficult to realize: why did he not settle in one of the Maldive islands, which number in the hundreds, and spend the rest of his life in peace and happiness? He knew very well that he could not do so, that his situation was different, and that the life he had chosen for himself was the complete opposite to the weaver's. Incidentally, Ibn Battuta was at that time on board a ship, with his womenfolk and his servants, having intended to seize power in the Maldives with the help of the king of Ma'bar's troops.

To live on an island, or in an isolated place, with a small family, means leading an ordinary life. This was the case with Ibn Battuta only once, before his journey, when he lived with his family in Tangier. Not coincidentally, when he mentioned his departure at the beginning of his travels, he used the image of "birds forsak[ing] their nests" (1958–2000, 1: 8). He left his original nest never to return. The island, for him, is a lost paradise to which there is no hope of returning.

He tried repeatedly and unsuccessfully to settle in this or that place. In Abadan, he visited an old shaikh and longed to stay with him: "I entertained the idea of spending the rest of my life in the service of this shaikh, but I was dissuaded from that by the pertinacity of my spirit" (2: 282–83). In a city in Yemen, he mixed with a group of fakirs who devoted themselves to worship and thought of joining them: "I should have wished to remain with them for the rest of my life, but my desire was not fulfilled" (2: 365). At Gibraltar, he entertained the same thought: "I would have liked to be one of those serving there till the end of my life" (4: 935).

Each time, he envies those who have chosen to settle down comfortably, but fails to follow their example or to resist the deep-seated urge to wander endlessly. Movement and stillness, wandering and settling, appearance and disappearance— two urges tearing him apart, although movement is the more powerful of the two; it is his desire and exalted goal. This is what the first shaikh he met prophesied, in Egypt: "I see that you are fond of traveling and wandering from land to land" (1: 23). Ibn Battuta affirms that with great pride: "I have indeed—praise be to God—attained my desire in this world, which was to travel through the earth, and I have attained in this respect what no other person has attained to my knowledge" (2: 282).

Despite many periods of stillness, he persisted in traveling and refused to stop—traveling, that is, to visit holy men, Sufi lodges, and shrines. In what capacity does he tour the earth? He often accompanied students and poor travelers, and in that manner he would stop and be accommodated at religious lodges. Sometimes, he was described as a jurisprudent. That was, on the whole, before he reached India, after which everything changed. He would continue to visit pious and holy men, but meeting them would become a secondary objective, for he entered a new phase of his life that revolved around the service of kings and sultans.

Surveying his journey, we notice that the transformation actually occurred before he reached India. There are indications that he wanted to meet and be close to kings. But he could only meet them once he left Arabic-speaking lands behind. When describing those countries, he reports on their kings but seldom meets them (he greeted the sultan of Yemen, who received the public on Thursdays). Amazingly, as soon as Ibn Battuta left the Arab countries, he began to be received and honored by sultans. Language difference has perhaps something to do with this phenomenon. Interestingly also, on his way back from his journey, he did not have the privilege of meeting the sultans of the Arab countries he passed through.[1]

---

1. He learned Persian and Turkish over the course of his travels.

As we know, he attained the greatest stature in India, where he remained for several years. He aimed to get there in order to enter the service of Sultan Muhammad Ibn Tughluq, as he admitted to the sultan's retinue: "They . . . asked me why I had come [to India]. I told them that I had come to enter permanently the service of Khund 'Alam [Master of the World],[2] namely the sultan" (3: 607). Noticeably, Ibn Battuta used the phrase "spending the rest of my life in the service of" when talking about the shaikh he visited in Abadan and with whom he wished to remain. Thus he moved from serving holy men to serving kings. In this way, we can divide his journey into two parts: the first part revolves around visiting shaikhs, and the second part around visiting kings.

At some point, then, the tendency to appear triumphed and the tendency to disappear waned and expired, leaving no doubt behind that it was only a whim or a wish that remained unrealized until other options were no longer available. Take, for example, what happened to Ibn Battuta in India. Its sultan appointed him judge in Delhi and showered him with money, but one day became angry and was about to punish him. "The Sultan gave orders that four of his slaves should remain constantly beside me in the audience-hall, and customarily when he takes this action with anyone it rarely happens that he escapes. . . . Some time later, I withdrew from the Sultan's service and attached myself to the shaikh and imam, the learned, devout, ascetic, humble-minded, pious Kamal ad-Din 'Abdallah al-Ghari. . . . I devoted myself to the service of this shaikh and gave my possessions to the poor brethren and the needy. There seemed to me

2. Probably a corruption of the Persian khudaawand-i 'alam (translator's note).

to be a certain sluggishness in me because of something which remained in my possession, so I rid myself of everything I had, little or much, and I gave the clothes on my back to a mendicant and put on his clothes" (3: 765–66).

Yet, as expected, soon he returns to the service of Muhammad Tughluq:

> When I had completed forty days the Sultan sent me saddled horses, slave girls and boys, robes and a sum of money, so I put on the robes and went to him. I had a quilted tunic of blue cotton which I wore during my retreat, and as I put it off and dressed in the sultan's robes I [did not recognize] myself.[3] Ever after, when I looked at that tunic, I felt a light within me, and it remained in my possession until the infidels despoiled me of it on the sea. When I presented myself before the sultan, he showed me greater favor than before, and said to me, "I have expressly sent for you to go as my ambassador to the king of China, for I know your love of travel and sightseeing." (3: 767)

To go from serving the shaikh to serving the sultan is to change clothes; and by taking off the cotton tunic, Ibn Battuta loses, as he puts it, his inner light and becomes someone else ("I did not recognize myself"). Interestingly, he tried, in a manner of speaking, to reconcile the two tendencies that pull him apart, so he traveled the earth with the robe until it was stolen from him.

Did he ever consider returning to his homeland? Did he long to be back in his birthplace, his nest, or the "island" on which he grew up? We may usefully recall here an incident that took place in China: "When I was in Sin Kalan I heard that there was

---

3. Gibb's translation reads, "I upbraided myself" (translator's note).

there a venerable shaikh over two hundred years old . . . and that he lived in a cave outside the city, giving himself to devotion. I went to the cave and saw him at the entrance. He was thin, very ruddy, showed the traces of his devotional practices, and had no beard. I greeted him; he took my hand, sniffed it, and said to the interpreter: 'This man is from one end of the world and we are from the other'" (4: 897). The old man identified Ibn Battuta's origin by smelling his hand, as though the land in which one is raised leaves an imprint on the skin, marking the body with an everlasting scent. Ibn Battuta's meeting with the old Chinese man is a meeting between the two ends of the world, the west and the east—a strange thing for the rising and the setting suns to meet simultaneously somewhere in China.

Despite Ibn Battuta's admiration for Chinese architecture and its brilliant, industrious people, he did not want to live among them: "China, for all its magnificence, did not please me. I was deeply depressed by the prevalence of infidelity and when I left my lodging I saw many offensive things which distressed me so much that I stayed at home and went out only when it was necessary. When I saw Muslims it was as though I had met my family and my relatives" (4: 900). The contrast between Islam and infidelity parallels that between inside and outside, and that between the familiar and the unfamiliar. The house stands for origin, what is familiar to Ibn Battuta and what he was raised on; staying indoors means protecting himself against the temptations of the outside world and clinging to conventional values. Oddly, Ibn Battuta speaks of withdrawing and recoiling within himself at the same time that he travels the length and breadth of China!

Perhaps the reference to home and family indicates a hidden desire to return to the land of origin, and significantly, this is the first time in the journey that such a desire finds expression. Immediately before speaking of home, Ibn Battuta recounts his meeting with someone from Ceuta who had settled in China:

> One day when I was in the house of Zahir al-Din al-Qurlani a big ship arrived belonging to one of the jurists most highly regarded by them. I was asked if I would receive him and they said: "Maulana Qiwam al-Din of Ceuta." I was surprised at his name but when we conversed after our formal greetings it occurred to me that I knew him. I looked at him for a long time. He said: "I see you looking at me as though you knew me." I said: "Which country are you from?" He said: "From Ceuta." I said: "I am from Tangier." He greeted me again and wept and I wept too." (4: 899)

Qiwam al-Din of Ceuta managed to blend into Chinese society, and despite the copious tears of nostalgia for his country, he apparently had no intention of returning to it. Ibn Battuta, however, could not or would not blend in, and his departure from China may have something to do with his failure to meet the great "khan," or sultan.

He left one end of the earth heading for the other end. Yet he was not entirely satisfied with that, for when he reached southern India, he considered contacting the sultan Muhammad Tughluq once again: "I wanted to return to Dihli [sic], but became afraid to do so" (4: 913). (The reason for his fear was that he had lost in a sea storm the gift that he had been charged with delivering to the sultan of China.) It is likely that he returned to Morocco after giving up the hope of gaining favor with the sultan of India or other sultans.

At any rate, he surely would not have recorded his travels had he not returned home. If we grant that one does not usually write a travelogue while away from home, Ibn Battuta's book would not have been written had he not returned to his family and relatives. There are some indications of that in what he says, for while in Constantinople, he asked the king "to designate someone to ride about the city with me every day, that I might see its wonders and curious sights *and tell of them in my own country*, and he designated such a guide for me" (2: 506). For Ibn Battuta, seeing Constantinople is not an end in itself; his main purpose is to tell his friends about it when he returns. The desire to travel is inseparable from the desire to narrate the journey. Wandering is of no great value if it does not turn into a narrative transmitted to listeners and readers.

In this way, Ibn Battuta's observations turn into stories, which, for example, he tells the king of Constantinople: "He questioned me about Jerusalem, the Sacred Rock, [the church called] al-Qumama, the cradle of Jesus, and Bethlehem, and about the city of al-Khalil (peace be upon him) [Hebron], then about Damascus, Cairo, al-'Iraq and the land of al-Rum, and I answered him on all of his questions. . . . He was pleased with my replies" (2: 506). What happens with the king of Constantinople is repeated with other kings. He tells them about his travels and the sultans he met, and describes to them the countries through which he passed. He became, in a sense, a wandering narrator.

Did Ibn Battuta contemplate writing his journey at that time? When he returned to Morocco, he told the story of his travels orally, and he may have been content with that method. Yet he tells us that he wrote down certain things: in Bukhara, he visited the tombs of the learned men, which are "inscribed with their names and the titles of their writings. I had copied a great many of these, but they were lost along with all that I lost when the Indian infidels robbed me at sea" (3: 554). As we know, the final version of the journey was written by Ibn Juzayy, but what has interested scholars is that he declares in the conclusion that he relied on an extended text by Ibn Battuta: "This completes the epitome I made of the composition of the shaikh Abu 'Abdallah Muhammad b. Battuta" (4: 977). We may regret the loss of that text, which represents the original version of the journey. But if it had survived, it would probably have had a documentary value at best, for Ibn Battuta had no literary training that would have allowed him to write well, which is the reason why he needed the help of Ibn Juzayy to write his journey.

In one respect, Ibn Juzayy summarized Ibn Battuta's text, and in another respect, he gave it a literary hue. In other words, he *translated* it. He depended on a written text dictated by Ibn Battuta at the command of Sultan Abu 'Inan: "A gracious direction was transmitted that he should dictate an account of the cities which he had seen in his travels, and of the interesting events which had clung to his memory" (1: 6). Most likely, what Ibn Battuta dictated lacked literary appeal, which led Abu 'Inan to command Ibn Juzayy to "assemble that which the Shaikh Abu 'Abudallah had dictated" (1: 6). Apparently, Ibn Battuta did not dictate the narrative of his travels to Ibn Juzayy directly, but to a scribe, and this dictation is what Ibn Juzayy edited, corrected, and gave a final form.

There are no further reports of Ibn Battuta following his dictation of the book. What did he do after that? We said that the struggle between movement and stillness in his trajectory was always resolved in favor of movement. Nevertheless, the idleness of his final years leads us to believe that stillness and disappearance triumphed in the end. Does that mean that, in fulfillment of an old wish, he withdrew to a hospice for Sufis or a small mosque to serve a shaikh until the end of his life? Did he finally manage to abandon the world and spend the rest of his life in devotion?

All we know, based on Ibn Hajar's report in *Al-Durar al-kaminah* [Hidden Pearls], is that Ibn Battuta died while serving as judge in an obscure Moroccan city. We can only assume that he managed to stay put, which he had failed to do earlier, and to remain silent, for there was no second Ibn Juzayy to recount what happened to Ibn Battuta during that period. And there need not have been, for the height of withdrawal is that no one remembers or seeks to identify you. If Ibn Battuta did not withdraw to a hospice or mosque, by taking up the position of judge in a remote place, he took refuge in an "island" similar to the one he once passed by, and where he found the weaver who had chosen a life of contentment and sufficiency.

5 ✦ Images

Had Ibn Battuta lived in the nineteenth century, it would not have occurred to him to travel to India or China, but most certainly to Europe, a continent that did not interest him and that he did not mention much in his *Travels*. Ironically, as one scholar has noted, the continent he turned away from discovered him and paid great attention to him (Dunn 1986, 317).

During his visit to Andalusia, he passed by the city of Marbella: "I found there a cavalry troop going to Malaqa [Malaga], and I wished to travel in their company. God Most High in His grace preserved me. They left before me and were taken prisoner on the road" (Ibn Battuta 1958–2000, 4: 939). Ibn Battuta escaped capture because of his tardiness, but the "enemy" lay in waiting for him for centuries, eventually taking him hostage in the nineteenth century, in 1853 to be exact, when the French translation of his *Travels* began to be published.

Throughout his wanderings in Asia and Africa, he saw strange things that surprised him, but only to a limited degree. The reason for that is that the explicit and implicit comparisons between his country and other countries are usually drawn along a vertical axis; that is, the phenomena he describes are either greater or lesser than what is common in Morocco. Thus, "The hens and cocks of China are very fat, fatter than our geese. Their hens' eggs are bigger than the eggs of geese among us. Their geese are not fat. We bought a hen which we wanted to cook but it would not fit into one pot; we used two. The cock in China is the size of an ostrich" (4: 889).

Painting, however, is a different matter: "No one, whether Greek or any other, rivals them in mastery of painting" (891). The Chinese are greater than the Europeans in this art form, but it is still possible to compare the two, whereas comparison is out of the question in the case of Morocco, where the phenomenon cannot be described along a vertical axis, but rather a horizontal one, that is to say an axis of fundamental difference that permits no comparison.[1] This explains Ibn Battuta's feeling of utter surprise at Chinese painting:

> One of the remarkable things I saw in this connection is that if I visited one of their cities, and then came back to it, I always saw portraits of me and my companions painted on the walls and on paper in the bazaars. I went to the Sultan's city, passed through the painters' bazaar, and went to the Sultan's palace with my companions. We were dressed as Iraqis. When I returned from the palace in the evening I passed through the said bazaar. I saw my and my companions' portraits painted on paper and hung on the walls. We each one of us looked at the portrait of his companion; the resemblance was correct in all respects. I was told the Sultan had ordered them to do this, and that they had come to the palace while we were there and had begun observing and painting us without our being aware of it. It is their custom to paint everyone who comes among them. They go so far in this that if a foreigner does something that obliges him to flee from them, they circulate

1. Explanation of those two axes can be found in Evelyn Birge-Vitz's article, "Type et individu dans l'autobiographie médiévale."

his portrait throughout the country and a search is made for him. When someone resembling the portrait is found, he is arrested. (4: 891–92)

Whereas the vertical axis is predominant in the classical travel narrative, it largely disappears in nineteenth-century texts describing Europe. What Rifaʿah Rafiʿ al-Tahtawi, Ahmad Faris al-Shidyaq, and others saw in France and England, respectively, is entirely different from what they had been used to in their countries, and thus their description falls mostly along a horizontal axis.[2]

On 13 December 1845, a Moroccan delegation left the city of Tetuan for France in order to deliver a letter from Sultan ʿAbd al-Rahman to King Louis-Philippe. Members of the delegation boarded a ship headed for Marseille, then took a carriage to Orléans, from where they rode the train to Paris, arriving on the 28th. During the fifty-three days they spent in the French capital, they were received by Louis-Philippe and other personalities, and they were able to see Parisian sights such as the Jardin des Plantes, the Pantheon, the Louvre, the Palais Royal, the Tuileries, in addition to Versailles. Throughout their sightseeing, they were accompanied by an interpreter named Alix Desgranges. When they returned to Morocco, a member of the delegation, Muhammad as-Saffar [d. 1881], recorded his observations and reactions.[3]

Needless to say, as-Saffar speaks of France, but he is also, directly or indirectly, speaking of Morocco. His compatriots

2. By the same token, the notion of "historical backwardness" had no meaning for Ibn Battuta, whereas it imposes itself, in one way or another, in the travel books of the nineteenth century.

3. *Sudfat al-liqaʾ maʿa al-jadid: Rihlat as-Saffar ila faransa*. I have benefited greatly from Susan Miller's introduction and notes to the text.

are his implied readers. From the first few lines of the book, a clear contrast emerges between "us" and "them"; he compares the two countries in everything he describes. Of course, when it comes to institutions and inventions unknown to Moroccans, such as trains, theater, telegraph, printing, newspapers, the two chambers, there can be no comparison. In such cases, as-Saffar assumes a pedagogical tone as he explains those innovations in detail, often starting with the phrase, "You should know that . . ." However, when he speaks of dress, currency, architecture, means of transportation, food, and table manners, he is able to compare, implicitly for the most part, since there is no need for him to remind his readers of what they know. Perhaps also he did not wish to make explicit comparisons to avoid making judgments that may be inappropriate or unfavorable to his compatriots.

As-Saffar went with the delegation because the sultan had ordered his ambassador, 'Abd al-Qadir Ash'ash, to take a scholar with him: "You should . . . take an 'alim [learned man of religion] to attend to religious matters such as prayers and reading from the Koran, for the French examine Muslims closely about the mysteries of their beliefs both in general and in particular" (as-Saffar 1992, 16).[4] As-Saffar's task is to satisfy the supposed religious curiosity of the French, a curiosity the origin and motives of which are not specified in the sultan's letter. Apparently, however, no one in France seemed to care about the religion of the Moroccan delegation. At least, no one on either side engaged the other in religious or theological debates. Nevertheless, an implicit disputation that is not without deceit forces itself on every page of the book.

4. For the text of the sultan's letter that 'Abd al-Qadir Ash'ash conveyed to France, see Miller 1992, 15–16.

What astonished as-Saffar were the images. As soon as he set foot in France, he was overwhelmed by a flood of paintings and statues. The crucifix was a stumbling block from the moment he saw it for the first time in Aix:

> "We saw a huge cross made of wood standing on one side of the town square. At its top was a smaller bit of wood made into the likeness of a crucified man, naked except for a cloth covering his maleness. What a sight it was! We were horrified to see it and thought that he was a criminal they had hung there, for without a doubt, whoever saw it [would think it] was a crucified man. I asked about this and they told me that it was the deity and the crucifix which they worshipped. They claim he is Jesus, that is to say, a likeness of him crucified. And there is no doubt that they believe in his divinity just as the Koran tells us, and there is no doubt about the untruth of their claim and the falsity of their belief" (1992, 108).

There are actually two shocks in this scene: on the one hand, as-Saffar and his companions reject the belief in Christ's crucifixion; on the other hand, a wooden image seemed to them like a person of flesh and blood ("We . . . thought that he was a criminal they had hung there"). Their horror may be justified, in any case, for it was the first time they had seen a crucifix or even a statue; as we know, sculpture requires a training of the gaze that the members of the delegation had not had. Yet this is not all, for this illusion recalls that which deceived Christ's enemies when they crucified someone else in his place.[5] The confusion

5. The Qur'an states that Christ was a prophet, not the son of God; that he was raised to heaven rather than crucified; and that someone else

of as-Saffar and his companions is similar to that of those who thought they had crucified Christ: in the first case, a wooden statue appeared to be a human being, and in the second, a man seemed to be Christ. It is as though the error that took place centuries before in Jerusalem is repeated in a town square in Aix.

To alleviate the shock, as-Saffar cites Qur'anic verses and sayings of the Prophet to emphasize that Christ was not crucified, then adds that throughout his stay in France he saw several paintings of Jesus and his mother Mary: "The figure of Jesus is portrayed in different ways: as a grown man, or a small boy in the lap or arms of Mary. In the church they pray to them both. . . . The proof of our eyes only increased our insight into their unbelief, the falsity of their creed, and the stupidity of their reasoning. Thanks be to God who guided us to the true religion" (1992, 110). Interestingly, he does not only reject images with religious themes but also those with worldly content. His distaste becomes particularly obvious when he visits the Louvre: "this huge and well-built palace would have been nicely decorated were it not for the many portraits which spoiled its beauty" (196).

In spite of that, "the worshipers of images, who believe in the Father and the Son," are strong, enjoying abundant resources, prosperity, and comfort. As-Saffar has no choice but to acknowledge that, and he asserts it on every occasion and in various ways. Of course, the memory of defeat at Isly (1844) is very much present in the book, if only implicitly. His agonizing sorrow unveils itself when the Moroccans are invited to watch a

---

was mistaken for him and crucified in his place (Qur'an 4:157–58, 5:73–75, 5:116–19, and elsewhere) (translator's note).

military parade: "their sultan summoned us to attend a review
of the troops as an extravagant expression of his high esteem for
us, for he does that only for those whom he holds in great favor.
But for us it was more a gesture of spiteful mockery" (1992,
190). Louis-Philippe accomplished what he had planned: "all
had passed, leaving our hearts consumed with fire from what we
had seen of their overwhelming power and mastery, their prepa-
rations and good training, their putting everything in its proper
place," in contrast to "the weakness of Islam, the dissipation of
its strength, and the disrupted condition of its people" (193–94).
On the way back, the Moroccans again felt their lowly position
when they passed through the city of Toulon, where they were
invited to board a battleship during war games and display of
strength, "which on the surface was festive, but underneath it
threatening and injurious. And yet, praise God, we do not fear
them, but fear only Him."[6] The bitter irony is that the same ship
had bombarded Tangier two years earlier, but as-Saffar did not
know that (120, n. 66).

In addition to comparing Morocco and France, as-Saffar
compares Muslims and Christians, and concludes that the
Islamic world is in a weak position. We sense his insistence on
the idea of the opposition between Islam and Europe, a subject that later on becomes extremely important. Yet he does not
name Europe. Did he see it merely as a stronghold of Christianity? Was Europe for him defined by its religion? He is hesitant
and unclear on this subject. Sometimes he ties the French, the

6. Miller translates this passage differently: "on the surface they mani-
fest nothing but pleasure, but inside they fear us as well as delight in us.
Praise be to God that we have no fear of them, for it is only God that we
fear" (as-Saffar 1992, 121) (translator's note).

object of his discourse, to Christianity, but at other times he separates their achievements from religion: "If you could see their conduct and their laws [at work], you would be profoundly impressed with them, despite their infidelity [*kufruhum*] and the extinction of the light of religion from their hearts" (194). Their religion does not explain their military superiority: "how capable [they are] in war and successful in vanquishing their enemies—not because of their courage, bravery, or religious zeal, but because of their marvelous organization, their uncanny mastery over affairs, and their strict adherence to the law" (194). This virtue is not only manifested in military affairs but also in other areas such as agriculture, trade, industry, and various aspects of social life.

In addition to their organizational ability, the French, according to as-Saffar, possess what we may call the will to knowledge and the desire to control time and space. He devotes a lengthy chapter to newspapers, in which "you will find the news from Paris and the rest of the land of the French; from all the lands of the Christians; from the lands of the East and the West; in fact, from everywhere" (151). He stresses that "the gazette is of such importance that one of them would do without food or drink sooner than do without reading the newspaper" (153). Along with the will-to-knowledge goes the will to accumulate and horde things that come from faraway places and from ancient times. In the Jardin des Plantes, as-Saffar wonders at the countless plants and animals that the French gathered from all continents, even from different epochs, and that he cannot name for the most part. He is embarrassed by his inability to name the things with which the Jardin des Plantes is filled, and the reason for his embarrassment is plain: the ability to name things signifies mastery over them; it means controlling the world.

Without expressing it, he suspects that there is a deep connection between their Jardin des Plantes and their "House of Books" (that is, what is now known as the Bibliothèque Nationale). In that space filled with knowledge and full of countless volumes, different languages and cultures exist side by side. The inclusion in the library, with such great care, of all the languages, or all the names, follows the same principle that explains the French passion for gathering the world's plant and animal species in the Jardin des Plantes. The same principle applies in other places where remnants of the past, such as coins and artworks, are kept. Thus, for as-Saffar, European culture is characterized by its greed and its fusion and digestion of foreign elements, which makes it an *impure* culture.

At the library, as-Saffar, who does not know French, finds that "some of them [the librarians] know Arabic, and if an Arab goes there, he will find someone who comprehends his words" (187). He leafed through several Arabic books there, including Imam Malik's *Muwatta'*, *Sharh al-'ayni 'ala al-jami' as-sahih*, and *Kashf az-zunun* (apparently he had not heard of this book before).[7] In this place, and outside of their usual context, those books seem to him like strangers who have lost their way. This feeling is confirmed when he sees "an enormous Koran in a single volume; two men had to carry it between them because of its size. It was in eastern script, and we had never seen anything approaching its beauty, splendor, and perfection. The gold and ornamentation on it were beyond words." It occurs to him that

7. These books, in the same order, are: "The Leveled Path" (the earliest book of Islamic law), "Al-'Aini's Commentary on al-Bukhari's *Sahih* (or collected sayings of the Prophet)," and Katib Çelebi's biographical dictionary, "The Reliable Guide to Books and Arts" (translator's note).

this copy of the Qur'an is out of place, like a hostage in the hands of the French, whereas "it should rightfully belong in the library of one of the kings of Islam, may God render them victorious and deliver it from the hands of the infidel." Nevertheless, he cannot but acknowledge that the Qur'an "is guarded extremely closely and [is harmed by nothing save the touch of idolatrous hands]" (188).[8]

The French enjoy all this power, wealth, and luxury, while those who follow the true religion are in a pitiful position! Faced with this contradiction, he had to ask the question, why them and not us?[9] The question is raised indirectly in the prologue to the book: "Praise be to God who separated all creation into monotheist and polytheist. . . . To some He gave a good life in this world, and for others He reserved the pleasures of the here-after" (74). He quotes the Qur'an when he and his companions are invited to Louis-Philippe's palace and are impressed by its splendor and magnificence. It is necessary in that situation to control the desires that comparison might arouse: "do not gaze longingly at what We have given some of them to enjoy, the finery of this present life: We test them through this" [Qur'an 20:131]. With the aid of the book of God, as-Saffar puts things in perspective, that is to say, on another plane, the plane of eternity. At that point, the world down below appears as a tantalizing illusion, a mirage. The French, as he describes them, are masters of deceptive appearances, for in addition to the care they lavish on the crucifix, they have a strong passion for mirrors: "The walls

8. Miller's translation reads, "and no one may touch it" (translator's note).
9. See Abdallah Laroui's comments on the travels of Ibn Idris and al-Kardudi in *Les origines sociales et culturelles du nationalisme marocain* [1977], 214–19.

were hung with great mirrors, taller than a man, which caught in the clarity of their glass the chandeliers and everything else, so that one imagined seeing a second room just like this one" (177).[10] When describing the stage set at the theater, he says that "all of it is drawn on paper, but to those who see it, there is no doubt that it is real" (144). In the conclusion to the book, after describing their great knowledge in the fields of commerce and finance, he once again quotes the Qur'an: "they only know the outer surface of this present life and are heedless of the life to come" [Qur'an 30:7].

At no time does as-Saffar recommend adopting the ideas of the French or learning from them, but his admiration of their technological achievements and their management of public affairs is obvious. At times, he even justifies some of their customs. Thus, when speaking of the theater, he makes a point of adding that "they claim that it is edifying for the spirit, instructive in morals, and restful for the body and soul" (as-Saffar 1992, 148). He also cites reports that the Prophet's apostles did not frown upon joking and laughter (it is not easy to discern whether he is trying to justify the theater or his description of it). More importantly, he talks about the Egyptians sent by "Muhammad Ali to learn the sciences one finds only there" (179–80). Does this not suggest that it would be useful to follow the Egyptian example? Is he not hinting to his leaders that they ought to send Moroccan students to be educated in France? We know that in his description of France he depends heavily on Rifa'ah al-Tahtawi's *Takhlis al-ibriz fi talkhis bariz* [Extracting

---

10. This recalls the Queen of Sheba's entry upon the prophet Solomon [Qur'an 27:44].

Gold in Describing Paris].[11] In comparison, al-Tahtawi appears bolder: he states without equivocation that his compatriots will not recover from their backwardness in the fields of science and industry until they learn from the Europeans, "for the excellence of those things in European countries is well-known and indisputable" (al-Tahtawi 2004, 61). In fact, Egypt, during Muhammad Ali's reign, had already proceeded on the path of reform.

As-Saffar does not offer the Moroccan government any direct advice related to educational, bureaucratic, or military reform. Yet despite this timidity and reserve, simply to write a book about his journey suggests that he thought reform necessary. In the prologue, he emphasizes that "it is wise for those who go far from home to record everything they see and hear, since they may find some knowledge and value in it. There is no better way of obtaining useful information than by mixing with people" (77). He also justifies writing his book by saying, "I am only doing it as a reminder to myself, and to inform others who may ask from among my fellow countrymen" (77–78). However, it seems that none of his countrymen asked him about anything, for his book (which in many respects reveals piercing insights into modernity) made no impact and was consigned to oblivion until it was recently discovered. Most probably, however, it will not tell readers anything new about France, but it will definitely tell them much about Morocco's condition in the mid–nineteenth century.

11. Al-Tahtatwi's book (1834/2004) is the first Arabic travel account of Europe in the modern (colonial) period (translator's note).

6 ✦ The Stage in Between

It does not appear that Ahmad Faris al-Shidyaq's [1804–87] position differs much from al-Saffar's, for in the introduction to *Kitab al-rihla* [The Book of Travels], al-Shidyaq has this to say about Europe: "As God is my witness, notwithstanding all the many strange and wonderful things I saw in those lands, I was ever depressed . . . to think about our country's lack of civilization, skill, and artistry comparable to theirs. But then I would find some consolation in thinking that our people are distinguished by their good character and generosity, which outshine shameful faults, and especially by their vigilance in guarding their honor against disgrace. Yet when I would go back to comparing the state of civic affairs, living standards, industrial skill, and the spread of education and public good, that consolation deserts me and my sadness returns" (1867, 155).

How did the imbalance between "our country" and "that country" come about? That question worries al-Shidyaq and causes his "grief over the low aspirations of his compatriots," especially when he remembers that "Muslims were the beacon of civilization and the arts in olden times, and they were role models in virtue and in all accomplishments."[1] Things have turned upside

---

1. For example, when speaking of the separation of powers in England, he says, "When are we ever going to be like those people? When will we learn our rights and responsibilities? Do you think that civilization means the law of the jungle? Absolutely not" (155).

down, so that the students (Europeans) have become the teachers, while the teachers (Muslims) have become the students, or rather, they are now obliged to learn from "those people." That is what prompted al-Shidyaq to write *Kitab al-Rihla*.[2] He will be the link between "his compatriots" and Europe. He will translate its achievements so that they could follow its example. What enables him to undertake this task is that "his affairs pull him right and left," that is, he has one foot here and one there.

Since he wrote poetry while in Europe, he must have pondered the situation of Arabic literature and its relation to European literature. That is what we will try to clarify based on his two books, *Al-saq 'ala al-saq fi ma huwa al-Fariyaq* [Al-Fariyaq's Crossed Legs] and *Kitab al-rihla*.

In *Al-saq 'ala al-saq*, we read that al-Fariyaq (a composite name, from Faris and al-Shidyaq) went from Malta, where he taught Arabic, to Tunisia for the summer vacation. "When al-Fariyaq was about to leave the city (Tunis), some of his acquaintances there said to him, 'If you were to praise its great governor, he would give you of his bounty, for he is most generous and beneficent.'" Upon returning to Malta, "it occurred to him to compose a poem in praise of the said governor, so he wrote a long poem . . . , and within mere days the said governor sent him a gift of diamonds" (Al-Shidyaq 1920, 2: 131–32). Al-Fariyaq praised the governor of Tunisia because he heard of his generosity. Herein we glimpse the nature of the traditional contract between the poet and the prince: a praise poem earns a reward.

After a while, al-Fariyaq was bored with teaching in Malta,

2. "My desire is to encourage my brethren to emulate those accomplishments" (3).

and it happened at that time that His Highness Ahmad Pasha, the great governor of Tunisia, went to France. He distributed a great amount of money to the poor in Marseille and Paris, among other cities, an act that generated much publicity, before he returned home. Al-Fariyaq thought to congratulate him in a poem that he sent to his Highness through a messenger. Within mere days, the captain of a warship knocked on his door. When he came in and took his seat, he said to al-Fariyaq, "Your poem reached our gracious Lord and he ordered me to bring you to him in the battleship." When he heard this, al-Fariyaq rejoiced at the relief that his craft promised to bring him. (2: 196–97)

This passage praises the governor of Tunisia, whose generosity extended to the poor in France. Yet what is interesting is that al-Fariyaq took his family with him to Tunisia, without incurring the governor's indignation as a result. "Here we must note the generosity with which God distinguished the Arabs among all other peoples. . . . If one of the notables of the Franks invited someone, and that person brought along with him somebody other than himself, he would be received badly, if at all" (2: 197–98). Praise for one Arab gradually turns into praise for all Arabs, the best mannered among God's creation, and denigration of Europeans, or the Franks, as they are called in the text, who turn you away from their door if you bring someone they did not invite.

What makes al-Fariyaq compare Arabs and Franks when speaking of the governor of Tunisia? The secret behind this digression will be revealed momentarily. For now, suffice it to say that al-Fariyaq moves with his family to Tunisia, "where he became acquainted with gracious and cultured people, some of whom entertained him and some provided generously for him. While there, he was privileged to kiss the hand of the exalted governor, from whom he attained abundant gifts" (2: 200). It is a happy period for al-Fariyaq in which everyone acknowledged and celebrated him. In other words, he acceded to the position of the pampered court poet, much like the poets of old, such as al-Mutanabbi.

Yet while he resided in Tunisia, something unexpected happened. The minister of state asked him, "Do you know the French language?" He replied, "No, Sir, I did not care to learn it, for as soon as I learned the English tongue, I forgot of my own an equal amount to what I had learned. My head was destined to contain a certain amount of knowledge; if it increases on one side, it decreases on the other" (2: 200). The conversation ends here without revealing to us the minister's reason for asking the question. It is a strange question, if we consider that it was never asked of an ancient poet. It would have never occurred to any vizier to ask a poet about his possible knowledge of a language other than Arabic. However, we learn from an undisclosed source that the minister intended to appoint al-Fariyaq to a position in his cabinet if the latter had known that language, and so we understand that al-Fariyaq, who had been bored with teaching Arabic in Malta, lost a precious opportunity in Tunisia because of his ignorance of French. Something had changed in the world; Arabs now need another language besides theirs. The governor of Tunisia is pleased with panegyric and he rewards it, but he only appoints someone who has mastered French to a position in his government. In a world ruled by the Franks, Arabic is no longer enough (even English, to which al-Fariyaq alluded, did not impress the minister, for well-known historical reasons).

Apparently, and in keeping with the playful mood prevailing in the text, al-Fariyaq did not learn French because he was afraid of losing Arabic, half of which he had forgotten when he learned English (throughout his travels, he always took al-Fiyruzabadi's *Al-qamus al-muhit* [Comprehensive Dictionary] with him).[3] Learning a foreign language comes at the expense of the native tongue. Al-Fariyaq forgot half of his Arabic when he learned English; if he were to learn French, only a quarter would be left of his Arabic. Here, there is probably an allusion to al-Jahiz's above-cited statement about the translator, which it would be well to recall at this point: "Whenever we also find him speaking two languages, we know that he has mistreated both of them, for each one of the two languages pulls at the other, takes from it, and opposes it. How could one tongue possibly manage two languages as it would only one?" (1996, 1: 76) Yet there is a difference between the situations of al-Jahiz and al-Shidyaq: al-Jahiz did not need to learn a language other than Arabic, whereas al-Shidyaq had to know one or more European languages.

Could al-Shidyaq have repeated his Tunisian experience in Europe? That seems impossible, for it would be unimaginable for an Arab poet to compose a poem in praise of a Frankish prince. Indeed, it would be unimaginable, in the nineteenth century, for any poet, whatever his language, to compose a panegyric, something that would have been anachronistic and Quixotic. Nonetheless, al-Shidyaq addressed such a poem to Queen Victoria: "I had praised the queen of the English in a poem and presented it to one of her officers, who turned it over to his wife to convey

3. Was his fear of losing Arabic what motivated him to write several books about it?

to some of the queen's ladies-in-waiting. I also translated it into their language. Until now, I have not received a response and do not know if it reached her" (1867, 302).

Did al-Shidyaq send his poem in both languages or only in English? All we know is that he waited several years in vain for a response from the queen or one of her courtiers. He took the trouble to translate the poem into English so as to facilitate communication, and he sought the help of an officer to convey it, but all this effort was in vain. The lesson he learned from this ordeal is this: "It is easier to write poems, whether in Arabic or in another language, than to present them to one of the Frankish kings." That is because "the Frankish kings are not accustomed to read poems in praise of themselves or other correspondence addressed to them. All of that is read by their secretaries, who answer as they see fit" (302). Did al-Shidyaq learn his lesson after his fruitless attempt to praise the Frankish kings? Not at all, for he praised Louis Napoleon after his coup of 2 December 1851: "My return to Paris coincided with the current sultan's assumption of political power as head of the Assembly at that time and his defeat of his jealous opponent. Some of my acquaintances advised me to praise him in a poem, for he was familiar with Arabic and many other languages" (300).

The reference to acquaintances came in exactly the same way earlier in connection with praising the governor of Tunisia. Al-Shidyaq suggests that he did not write the poem on his own initiative, but was advised to do so by someone he does not identify—under outside pressure, as it were. Should we believe him when he declares that he did not take the initiative? The question goes beyond al-Shidyaq to an age-old convention of writing: most ancient writers relate at the beginning of their works that somebody asked them to write a book on a certain subject, somebody who usually remains anonymous and who may be in a position of authority or merely a friend. This convention gives us the impression that writing was for them a very serious matter, and that they needed to shield themselves behind some authority in order to begin. In that sense, writing is not so much the result of a personal decision as a response to an insistent outside voice, something absolute that cannot be ignored.[4]

Napoleon's knowledge of Arabic corresponds to al-Shidyaq's knowledge of French (which he studied while in Paris)—a correspondence worthy of note. Poet and prince are both "familiar with many languages," and yet there is a wide gap between them, the gap that separates Arabic and European literary discourses. Al-Shidyaq's poem consists of sixty verses, and begins with an introductory *ghazal* of thirteen verses. Needless to say, this introduction is required, despite some poets' resentment of it.[5] The ancients (for example, Ibn Qutaybah) attempted to justify it by claiming that the *nasib* creates a good impression on the person being praised and disposes him to appreciate and enjoy the poem. Al-Shidyaq says that the introductory *ghazal* "is actually a strange convention of the Arabs. The eminent scholar al-Dasuqi said, 'You should know that poets are accustomed, when praising someone, to begin with love so as to stir up their talent,

4. See my book *Al-maqamat*, 147 ff. [In French, *Les séances*, 177–78].

5. This introduction, called *nasib*, in which the poet addresses or describes his beloved, was a standard feature of the pre-Islamic Arabic ode and came to be regarded as a required part of a formal poem until the early twentieth century. *Ghazal* is a general word for love poetry, but it can also be used to refer to *nasib* when used in the phrase "introductory *ghazal*," as Kilito does here (translator's note).

to rouse the poetic spirit through hyperbolic description, and to entertain and exercise the mind'" (303).

From previous experience, al-Shidyaq had sensed the strangeness of this convention: "When Monsieur Ducat translated my poem in praise of the late Ahmad Pasha-Bey, the governor of Tunisia, and published it with the translation, some people asked me if the Pasha's name was Su'ad, since I open the poem with 'Su'ad visited me when darkness drew its veil.' I said, 'No, that is a woman's name.' The questioner responded, 'What does the woman have to do with you and the Pasha?'" (303). For a European, the woman is an intruder in a praise poem who sneaks in between two men, the praiser and the praised, and meddles in something that concerns only men.

Even though he was not convinced of the necessity of starting the poem with an introductory *ghazal*, al-Shidyaq could not avoid it without being faulted by his rivals and peers. That is because the poem, while intended for Louis Napoleon, was also addressed to critics and connoisseurs of poetry who would, in the end, be the ones to judge it. In that sense, the poem has two intentions and two audiences: Napoleon and his court on the one hand, and potential Arab readers on the other. Therefore, the poem has two contradictory objectives: if he were to satisfy the Arab reader with the introductory *ghazal*, al-Shidyaq would doubtless for the same reason displease the European reader, for he knows that "nothing is more repugnant for the Franks than a praise poem that describes a woman as having a narrow waist, heavy buttocks, large eyes, noble height, and so forth, since all of their poetry is castrated.[6] Worse than that is to describe the

---

6. *Lisan al-'arab* [a major dictionary of classical Arabic] states, "castrated poetry: that which lacks *ghazal*."

beauty of a boy. Worse and worse is to give feminine attributes to a man" (303).

How does al-Shidyaq attempt to reconcile Arabic and European tastes? He begins his poem by criticizing the convention imposed on the poet:

> Lovers' custom is to sing profusely their love
> Before their praise, or weep at abandoned campsites.
> Yet no! No beauty occupies my thoughts,
> For the fair one's heart knows no constancy.
> My passion is a vision in a dream,
> Which ere it appeared I had not known. (300)

Oddly enough, al-Shidyaq emphasizes, in these lines, that he is against traditional *nasib*, yet he immediately turns to praising a beautiful woman. Denial leads to affirmation. This hesitation between negativity and positivity is reflected in the image of the woman he sings about—she is a vision, an unreal, illusory visitor, a mere dream. Al-Shidyaq could not banish woman from the poem, so he turned her into a phantom that appears in his sleep, an apparition in the dead of night.

Boasting of his skill and mastery of the art of poetry, al-Shidyaq declares that he "composed this poem in one day." Yet "the remaining difficulty was in presenting it to the person it praises" (302)—for surely the poem would be useless scribbling if it did not reach Napoleon.

> I met with the dear, sensible, and cultured friend the *kha-waja*[7] Rafael Kahla and asked his opinion. He said, "I know of a way to convey it to him, but we should translate it into

---

7. A title for Europeans or Christians (translator's note).

French. Its meaning will not be lost in translation because the poem is composed after their manner—except perhaps for praising the apparition. But that is a minor thing, given that at the beginning of the poem you disparage the introductory *ghazal* in a praise poem." So we translated it and showed it to one of their men of letters who said, "It is better to present it untranslated, since the sultan has translators who can do that for him." Accordingly, it was presented as it is. (303–4)

Apparently, the French littérateur was not satisfied with the two friends' translation, so he advised them to present the original. Thus, contact with Napoleon would not be direct but through his translators. "A few days later, the postman knocked on the door and delivered a letter from the sultan addressed to the above-mentioned *khawaja* and myself, to the effect that the poem reached his Royal Highness, who was pleased with it, with many thanks" (304).

That was all. The matter was concluded with a letter addressed to the two partners. In contrast to Queen Victoria, Louis Napoleon (or his secretary) took the trouble to respond to the poem. Did al-Shidyaq expect more? He denies that: "My sole intention was to enrich my poetry collection, as poets do, so that it would be said of them, 'He said this in praising the king and that in praising the prince'" (302). He longs for the prestige of poets whose poetry collections include the names of the mighty. Yet he pretends to forget that poets are also in the habit of composing praise poems in order to receive gifts and awards. Was that not the case with the governor of Tunisia, who sent a warship to escort and honor him? At any rate, he received nothing from Louis Bonaparte, not an invitation or even an audience.

This must have pained al-Shidyaq, for he kept waiting for the opportunity to make contact once more and to remind Louis Bonaparte of his debt. The "sultan" did not reward the praise poem, and that is a breach of the traditional relationship between poet and prince. The opportunity presented itself to al-Shidyaq a year later when Louis Napoleon restored the empire and took the name Napoleon III: "At that time, the said sultan assumed the reins of power and was declared Emperor, so I was tempted again by 'and he said in praise of . . . ' to congratulate him with a poem that I would present to him through his chief translator, the Count Degranges" (304). The new poem consists of thirty verses (half the length of the first one) of nothing but praise, that is, without *nasib*. It begins with "Louis Napoleon is entitled to sovereignty / And kingship, unrivaled he is in greatness." By abandoning the introductory *ghazal* and embarking on praise from the first line, al-Shidyaq thought that he had removed the greatest obstacle between him and the one he praises. In order to secure the acceptance of his poetry, he disrupted the familiar order of the poem, repudiated woman entirely, and denied her her rightful place at the beginning of a praise poem. He amputated his poetry, castrated it so as to approximate European taste.

But was that enough? Not at all, and that became clear when he read his poem to the chief translator: "He said, 'None of the qualities you attribute to the sultan is specific to him alone; they apply equally to any king'" (304). Al-Shidyaq's words are too general to fit Napoleon exactly; they reflect the image of all kings and none specifically. Napoleon would not find himself in them. In that sense, the Arabic poem robs the object of praise of his particularity, so he is lost within an ideal type in which all images merge. This explains a phenomenon to which Arab critics of old alluded, namely that some poets praised several kings with one poem. If the poem fits each of them, why go through the trouble of composing new verses every time? A poet need only compose one poem, which he would recite before all the kings he visits.[8]

Moreover, there is a linguistic and cultural barrier to understanding, which is what the chief translator indicated to al-Shidyaq: "The poem is abstruse and untranslatable. If you present it as it is, it would be appreciated for nothing more than the handwriting and the form on the page" (304). If the poem drew this reaction from someone who is well versed in Arabic, then how would ordinary readers feel? It would become mere scribble to all of them, starting with Napoleon. They would look at it as glyphs engraved on the walls of an ancient temple, obscure symbols that no one save archaeologists, or in this case Orientalists, could understand.

Al-Shidyaq was not unaware of this dissimilarity between Arabic and European literatures, with which he was familiar. He recounts that he was aware of this situation before composing his first poem in praise of Napoleon. He knew that the Franks

> rejected the exaggerated description of the person being praised. When they praise someone, they address the reader and make it a sort of history, so they mention his goals, his endeavors, and his precedence over the kings who came before him and whom they list. As for comparing him to the sea, or to clouds, or to a lion, or to a mountain, or to the full moon, or to a sword, they find all of that banal. They do not attribute

8. See the chapter on "The Polyandrous Ode" in Kilito's *The Author and His Doubles*, 24–33 (translator's note).

generosity to him, or say that his gifts reach those far and near to him, for their praise is addressed to the public and not to the person praised. And despite my knowledge of this situation, I could not resist the Arab poet's urge to present the said poem to Napoleon, especially when I heard that he knows our language. (306)

The difference between praise in the two literatures is the nature of the contract between praiser and praised. Arabic praise is based, as indicated earlier, on a personal contract between poet and prince, according to which a poem is presented in exchange for a reward. As for European praise, the contract is between the author and "the public"—that is, general readers—and, therefore, generosity is not mentioned in it, since the praiser does not expect a reward. The one praised is addressed directly in the first case, while in the second he is spoken of in the third person.

If al-Shidyaq could not resist the desire to present the first poem to Napoleon, he was persuaded by the chief translator's reasoning concerning the second poem: "Therefore, I refrained from presenting it and thanked him for his advice. But I do not refrain from including it here so as to swell the size of this book" (304). The poem will not be lost completely, since it will go to the Arab reader, who is the last refuge after the European reader turned away from it. Al-Shidyaq falls back on his own people after being denied by the foreigners, who returned his poetry to him with kindness mixed with some disdain.

Al-Shidyaq recounts this experience several years after the fact, which may explain his satirical tone and aloof attitude. It does not take much to imagine his disappointment at his complete failure to extract recognition for his poetry from the Franks. However, the matter extends beyond his personal sensitivity to Arabic poetry in its entirety. Al-Shidyaq's two poems stand in metonymic relationship to Arabic poetry, and their rejection is a rejection of all of Arabic poetics. Consequently, it is a rejection of Arabic literature, the most important component of which is poetry. Outside of its familiar sphere, Arabic literature has no currency—indeed, has no existence. As far as al-Shidyaq is concerned, this violent rupture between Europe and the Arab world is a double humiliation, personal as well as cultural.

We find no intimations of this feeling in his book, *Kashf al-mukhabba*, which was written some time after the incident, in 1857.[9] The wound had not healed before that date and was still bleeding in *Al-saq 'ala al-saq*, which was published in 1855, three years after the composition of the second praise poem. In that book, al-Shidyaq freely vents his anger at the Franks while describing the honors with which he was received in Tunisia:

> Who of their kings would send a warship to escort a poet and then load him with money and precious gifts? Upon my life, whoever praises their kings receives nothing but ridicule. Even so, they are the most desirous of praise and gratitude among all creation. Yet they disdain being praised by a poet who

9. *Kashf al-mukhabba 'an funun urubba* [Uncovering the Arts of Europe] is the second volume of *Kitab al-rihla* [The Book of Travels]. The first volume is titled *Al-wasita ila ma'rifat malta* [The Guide to Malta]. For an account of the composition of the two volumes, see Muhammad al-Hadi al-Matwi, *Ahmad Faris al-Shidyaq: Hayatuh wa atharuh wa ara'uhu fi al-nahda al-'arabiyya al-haditha* [Ahmad Faris al-Shidyaq: His Life, Works, and Views on the Modern Arab Renaissance] (Beirut: Dar al-maghrib al-islami, 1989), 1: 197–99.

seeks a reward from them. . . . None of Frankish poets ever deserved to be his king's confidant, the greatest boon for them being to be permitted to recite their poetry in some entertainment. (1920, 2: 198–99)[10]

He then adds,

Therefore—that is, because generosity is a special quality of the Arabs—no other nation produced poets as great as they did in all ages and places, from pre-Islamic times till the end of the caliphate and the Arab state. The Greeks boast of one poet, Homer; for the Romans, it is Virgil; for the Italians, Tasso; for the Austrians, Schiller;[11] for the French, Racine and Molière; for the English, Shakespeare, Milton, and Byron. But the Arab poets, who are greater than all of those, are countless. Indeed, in the age of the caliphs, and under each one of them, perhaps two hundred poets emerged, all excellent and outstanding. (1920, 198)

To whom does al-Shidyaq address this talk? To the Arabs, whom he regards as the most generous of all people, and consequently, those with the most poetry. If the Franks excel in "civilization," Arabs have the greater prestige in poetry. Yet something remains hidden and unspoken in his discourse, since the Arab poets of whom he is proud emerged in a remote past, "in the age of the caliphs"; poetry represents the Arab past, whereas civilization characterizes the Frankish present. Then there is a more complicated issue: who says that the Arabs excel

---

10. The reference is probably to plays performed at court (translator's note).

11. This is actually a German poet.

over others in poetry? Who accords them that pride of place? Al-Shidyaq does not base his opinion on any Frankish authority, that is to say, he does not cite any European source in support of this categorical judgment. He acknowledges what the Franks have accomplished "of civilization, skill, and invention," but the Franks acknowledge neither his own poetry nor Arabic poetry in general. Indeed, what he relates of their judgment on the style of the Arabic poem indicates their distaste for it; they find it awful, at least in some of its aspects.[12]

12. Times and circumstances have changed, but one thing has not: whenever Arabs listen to a line of poetry, they are enraptured, moved to liberality, and transported with joy, just like their ancestors. They may sacrifice everything except their poetry; they regard themselves as poets, above all. Nevertheless, their poetry has not found its way to Europe; apart from specialists, no European could name an Arab poet today. This is not only true of present-day Europeans, but in the past as well. Cervantes regarded Arabs primarily as storytellers, and there is no stronger evidence of that than his attribution of his novel *Don Quixote* to an invented Arab historian, Cide Hamete Benengeli. This attribution means that Cervantes believed that the origin of storytelling, of the novel, is Arab. Yet the remarkable thing, aside from the ascription of the narrative to an Arab writer, is his characterization of Arabs as liars. Yes. Arabs, according to him, are congenital liars; they invent stories; they lie as they breathe. This trait allows them to excel in the art of storytelling. On that view, Europeans were bound to take interest in Arabic narrative. Consequently, in the early eighteenth century, Galland translated *The Thousand and One Nights* into French. Significantly, in that translation, he paid no attention to the poetic verses in the book, and did not bother to translate them. He apparently regarded Arabic poetry as inconsequential and insignificant, and narrative as the quintessential Arabic art form. In general, Westerners' interest in *The Thousand and One Nights*, from Galland to Borges, supports the belief that what distinguishes the Arabs is narrative and narrative alone.

And it is not only the Franks, for in the context of describing the silence with which his praise of the English queen was met, al-Shidyaq says, "Any Turkish notable who learns the languages of the Franks follows in their path. I composed another poem in praise of Wali Pasha, the High Port's ambassador to Paris, and another addressed to Namiq Pasha, and another to Muhammad Pasha Ali, and none of those poems resulted in good or ill" (1867, 302). The stance of those Turkish notables toward al-Shidyaq's poetry (and Arabic poetry?) is similar to that of the English and the French. In al-Shidyaq's opinion, they are to be excused to some extent, for their behavior results from their learning European languages, which leads them to adopt those people's customs and tastes, such that the praise poem appears to them as a deserted and collapsing structure. If this trend continues, the infection will no doubt shortly spread to the Arabs.

Immediately after saying that he refrained from presenting his second poem to Emperor Napoleon III, al-Shidyaq moves to a different but related topic: "At that time, I began to write the book of al-Fariyaq" (306), meaning *Al-saq 'ala al-saq*. Why this passing reference? What compensation did he seek in writing that book? What is the secret of his switching from verse to prose, from composing praise poems to writing a book about . . . what? Let us set aside the matter of classifying the book as a journey, novel, or autobiography in the third person and suffice it to raise this question: What could an Arab writer who had seen Europe in the mid–nineteenth century and noticed the wide gulf separating it from his familiar world say? What could he write when he sees to his chagrin that the literature that nurtured him does not satisfy European taste? What is left for him when he realizes, consciously or unconsciously, that his native culture belongs to the past, while that of Europe is synonymous with the present? He will certainly not betray his past and will not waste any opportunity to declare his allegiance to it, yet at the same time he has no choice but to envision the future of the Arabs in Europe's present. That being the case, he will describe his predicament by holding endless comparisons between the two worlds, the two epochs—or, if we prefer, between the two legs. Indeed, he will cross one leg on the other and sink into contemplation of his situation and his place. As a thirteenth-century German poet said (apparently in reference to the disintegration of the chivalric age):

> I sat on a rock,
> And crossed my legs,
> Rested my elbow on my knee,
> And in my open palm I held
> My chin and cheek.
> There I pondered long
> How one should live in this world.
>
> [Walter von der Vogelweide]

7 ✦ Thou Dost Not, and Shalt Not, Speak My Language

I do not recall who said (and how I wish it was I who said it) that "we are the guests of language." It is a beautiful expression that indicates that we reside in it, enjoying its bountiful gifts. Of course, during our residence in its realm, that is, throughout our lives, we assume the respectful manners required of guests toward their host.[1] However, sometimes it seems to me that the speaker is the host and that language is the guest—a quarrelsome and stubborn guest who arrives uninvited and who takes possession of the host and inhabits him against his will.[2] We are inhabited, or haunted, by language, as though by a supernatural force. This impression of mine is confirmed when I see people speak a foreign language that I do not understand; perplexed for a moment, I almost come to think that they are lost in their language, unable to escape from it, that no one can free them from its clutches, that their condition has no remedy.

1. *Adab* in Arabic means both "good manners" and "literature." The metaphor of the guest, as Kilito uses it, is, therefore, not fully translatable: to be a well-mannered guest of language signifies learning the norms and tastes associated with literature in that language (translator's note).

2. In Arabic and French, the two languages in which Kilito writes, the word for "language" (*lughah, langue*) is a linguistic feminine, and so the "guest" in this sentence is a female. The significance of this will become clear from the example Kilito gives later in the chapter (translator's note).

One day I realized that I dislike having foreigners speak my language. How did that happen? I used to think of myself as an open-minded, liberal person who wished unto others what he wished unto his kin. Furthermore, I used to think it my duty to endeavor as best I could to make my language radiate its brilliance, to increase the numbers of its learners, and so forth. But that noble goal disappeared when I realized that I dislike having foreigners speak my language. That dislike had actually been there all along, except that I had not been aware of it and dared not confess it to myself, let alone to others. Incidentally, literature often saves us from loneliness, in that it helps to rid us of our unwholesome, shameful thoughts, or rather, it makes us conscious of them and allows us to contemplate them. Some thoughts, which seem to us reprehensible, obscene, unspeakable, we chance to find expressed by this or that author, and right away they lose their private character and become common to many people.

Speak my language or be silent: it is by and large a common condition. Why do you not speak as I speak? Why is your tongue different from mine? In moments of exhaustion, I may become angry and frustrated at someone who does not know my language, and I may even go so far as to think it his fault, that out of deliberate rudeness he speaks another language just to ridicule and spite me. What is worse is that I may feel this anger even when the person speaks the same language I speak: it is enough for him to use poetic or philosophical expressions that I do not understand to make me uneasy; I find his speech intolerable and feel that nothing justifies the least effort on my part to fathom its meaning, if it has any. In this connection, I recall a sentence from one of al-Hariri's *maqamat*: Abu Zayd al-Suruji and his son came before a certain judge and spoke to him unintelligibly, so he replied, "Make yourselves clear or disappear." Speak plainly or get out of my sight.

In a detective novel by the American writer Donna Leon that takes place in Venice, the police commissario, Brunetti (a character that recalls Maigret, the protagonist of several novels by Georges Simenon), visits a singer, Signora Flavia Petrelli, in the course of investigating a murder case. He finds with her a young woman, and this delightful dialogue ensues:

> "I'd like to speak to you about the death of Maestro Wellauer."
> He glanced across the room to the other woman and added,
> "And speak to you too...."
>
> "Brett Lynch," the singer supplied. "My friend and secretary."
>
> "Is that an American name?" he asked the woman whose name it was.
>
> "Yes, it is," Signora Petrelli answered for her.
>
> "Then would it be better if we were to speak in English?" he asked, not a little bit proud with the ease with which he could switch from one language to the other.
>
> "It would be easier if we spoke in Italian," the American said, speaking for the first time and using an Italian that displayed not the least accent. His reaction was entirely involuntary and was noticed by both women. "Unless you'd like to speak in Veneziano," she added, slipping casually into the local dialect, which she spoke perfectly. "But then Flavia might have trouble following what we say." It was entirely deadpan, but Brunetti realized it would be a long time before he'd flaunt his English again.
>
> "Italian, then," he said. (Leon 1992, 25–26)

Brunetti was not pleased that the foreigner spoke his language. He was confused, embarrassed, and disappointed to discover that she not only spoke Italian as fluently as he did, but also the Venetian dialect. She is not expected to speak my language! This surprise may turn into resentment: Why does she speak my language? And it may turn into provocation and threat: Dare not speak my language! It is a rare case, and it may seem eccentric and puzzling. What happened to Brunetti with the American woman remained within the bounds of civility, with a touch of humor; he received her within the space of the Italian language, if only grudgingly. Despite his confusion, it did not occur to him to force her to speak English; he would not imagine, nor would we imagine him, censoring her use of Italian. Such censorship would be irrational, impermissible. How could I prevent a foreigner from using my language? However, what may be unexpected and difficult to imagine did happen one day, if we believe what the German writer [Francis] Schuldt reports in this regard:

In the early sixties, before China cut its relations with the Soviet Union, Peter and Mary Mayer, who were from London, taught English in a small Chinese city of about one or two million inhabitants. The only other foreigners left there were two Russian engineers, with whom they conversed from time to time at receptions and other semi-official occasions. One day, the English couple were summoned by the secret police for a lengthy interrogation the motives and purpose of which remained obscure at first. Eventually, the incriminating evidence came out. "Each time you talk to the Russians in public, you use Chinese. Therefore, you must be hiding something."

The Mayers protested their innocence and explained to the zealous secret police officers time and again that the Russians do not speak English and that they, in turn, do not know Russian, so Chinese is the only way for them to communicate. This, however, failed to convince the Chinese, who refused to be duped. "You are foreigners, just like the Russians, and can, therefore, speak foreign to them. But since you do not, there must be something fishy." (Kelly 1995, 77–78)

In using Chinese, the English become an object of suspicion. If they had "spoken foreign," if they had talked to the Russians in English or in Russian—that is, in a language other than Chinese—they would not have caused concern. But now they are under suspicion simply because they have spoken the local language. The total comprehensibility and complete clarity resulting from using the language everyone around them speaks became the height of ambiguity. Instead of being a sign of acclimation and integration, using Chinese became a token of division and schism, as though the foreigners meant harm and used Chinese to hide a terrible secret. Make yourselves unclear or disappear!

Despite its eccentricity bordering on caricature, this extreme case seems to me significant. It points to the desire to protect one's language from the insolence of others. Is that an exceptional case?

That is what seems at first. Indeed, are we not delighted to hear a foreigner speak our language? Do we not welcome and sympathize with his effort to express himself to us? Do we not encourage him to persevere in his struggle? In fact, it is a matter of effort and struggle, something that is obvious whenever he speaks. His pronunciation is crooked, his diction is haphazard, his sentences are irregular. He does not open his mouth without sending this message: I am a stranger, not one of you. He is, in short, pitiful; he evokes in us the noble desire to offer assistance, encouragement, and support.

But what if this stranger speaks exactly, and expresses himself as clearly, as we do? Everything changes in that case. Gentleness and kindness end, and suspicion begins. This person who came from a faraway place causes confusion, not only because he undermines our sense of superiority but also because he suddenly robs us of our language, the principle of our existence, what we consider to be our identity, our refuge, ourselves. This explains why Brunetti was disturbed when the American woman spoke to him in flawless Italian. He suddenly felt that a foreigner stole from him his language, his being, what makes him unique, and what he regards as his own. She occupied his language as though it were her own dwelling, thereby usurping his place of refuge. That led to his fear and his sense of being duped—his sense of the uncanny.

I had the same feeling when a Moroccan friend introduced me to an American student who had been living in Morocco in order to learn the dialect. I began to speak to her in it, slowly and with a pedagogical tone, carefully enunciating to make it easy for her to understand. But when she answered me, I realized from her first sentence how ironic the situation was. I was ashamed of having talked to her as though she were a small child who was learning to speak. Her spoken Arabic was excellent and without a blemish; in fact, she was able to pronounce letters that bother most non-Arabs, who fail to produce them, such as the qaf, the ʿayn, and the ḥa'. I was surprised, and for the first time I felt that my language is slipping away from me, or rather that the American woman had robbed me of it. Fortunately, I did not speak to her in standard Arabic, for if she spoke that, too, which was not unlikely, what would have been left for me?

The crowning touch was that, in the course of her speech, she used the expression *wallahila*. At that point, my Moroccan friend could not help herself and broke into uncontrollable laughter—mad, hearty laughter. Each time she tried to stop, it broke out anew. Why this laughter? If laughter required collusion and solidarity, I, too, must have laughed. When I now try to explain the shock that triggered laughter, I can come up with only two explanations. First, *wallahila* is a purely Moroccan expression that I have never heard from a non-Moroccan Arab; it is as though using it were an exclusive right to Moroccans and forbidden to others. So how could it pass on a European or American tongue that acquired Arabic as a foreign language? Second, the American woman used this expression—how shall I say?—so innocently and with the same ease that characterized the rest of her speech. Did she realize that *wallahila* contains the word "Allah," and that she let herself so easily tread on rough terrain? She referred, probably without knowing it, to a faith that apparently was not hers. I leave this question open.[3]

Let us return to Brunetti. He goes so far in welcoming the American woman as to offer to speak to her in English (he invited himself into the realm of that language). At the same time, he is happy to have the opportunity to show off his mastery of another language. Whatever the case, he assumes that the American woman does not know Italian. Why this hasty and reckless assumption? Why this "unleavened opinion," as

---

3. It is certainly the case that, in the meeting of languages, the desire to imitate causes such ironic situations, something that we often find in the writings of al-Jahiz and Ahmad Faris al-Shidyaq.

al-Jahiz would put it? Does he think that Americans are not interested in foreign languages? Does he think that, given the power relations among countries and languages, Americans do not need to learn Italian, whereas Italians would gain by learning English? Whatever the case, he presents himself as an Italian who speaks English; he also presents himself as a tolerant, generous person when he offers to forsake his Italian temporarily and to take on a different guise so as to come closer to the foreign lady.

Yet the latter refuses to receive or welcome him in the space of her language, and turns him back pitifully to his Italian. She is the one who forsakes her language and suddenly takes on a new guise. Moreover, as we have seen, she has not only mastered Italian, but also the Venetian dialect, Brunetti's. In addition to that, she coquettishly pays attention to her companion, the singer Flavia, who does not know that dialect. She will, therefore, not speak Venetian and content herself with Italian in order not to exclude Flavia from the conversation. Thus the lines of collusion and solidarity shift: the American woman steps forward as Brunetti's sharer in the Venetian dialect, which is unknown to the singer, whereas Brunetti believed that the singer was his sharer in the Italian language, which he thought the American did not know.

That is not all. When the American woman decides that it is better to speak Italian, what does she mean? Perhaps this: since we are in Italy, let us speak Italian; in that sense, she suggests speaking that language out of courtesy. But perhaps the suggestion implies something else; perhaps she means to intimate to Brunetti that despite his knowledge of English, he does not know it, and will not know it, as well as she knows Italian. And assuming that he knows English well, he no doubt speaks it with an accent, while she is able to speak Italian without one. In that sense, she asserts her superiority to him, for she has the choice of language and the last word is hers. The battle will, then, be fought on his ground, in a region that he considers to be his alone; she has advanced to his position, besieged him, and put him in a very critical situation. By preventing him from speaking English, she humiliates him, cuts off his tongue, strips him of his arrogance, or—as some would say—of his manhood. She castrates him, especially when he probably intended to impress her by offering to speak in English.

In the final analysis, he is doubly robbed. On the one hand, she does not allow him to speak her language, and on the other, she storms into his language, invades and captures it. He is no longer the lord of his house, and he has no way of penetrating into hers. He is on the threshold, waiting for the unlikely chance to exact revenge. He wanted to impress her, but she impressed and entrapped him. He wanted to take on a new guise, wear a new garment, but she was the one who metamorphosed and shed her skin. He lost the paradise of his language—but when did he ever possess it?

Epilogue

Abu-Hayyan al-Tawhidi hated Matta ibn Yunus and once said about him, "He used to dictate a page for one dirham while stupefied with drink. He was sarcastic and pleased with himself, although he was the greatest and the basest of losers" (n.d., 1: 107). We must treat this statement with caution, for al-Tawhidi is the greatest satirist known in Arabic literature, and his tongue may even be considered sharper than al-Hutay'ah's. Yet when we read Matta's translation of the *Poetics* [tenth century], we cannot help cleaving toward what Abu-Hayyan says about him. It is a poor, repellent translation, not unlike the ravings of drunks and madmen.

No one today forgives Matta ibn Yunus for translating "tragedy" as panegyric and "comedy" as satire. Still, we may wonder if another translation was within his reach at that time.[1] Besides,

---

1. In this context, we may compare Rifa'a Rafi' al-Tahtawi's attempt to define theater: "I do not know of an Arabic word that renders the meaning of *spectacle* or 'theater.' The basic meaning of the word *spectacle* is 'view,' 'recreation ground' or some such, whereas 'theater' originally meant 'game,' 'entertainment,' or the venue where this takes place. And so it may be compared with those actors called 'shadow players.' More appropriately, shadow play is a form of theater" (al-Tahtawi 2004, 228). [Translator's note: *khayal al-dhil*, which literally means "shadow reflection"—or "shadow play," as al-Tahtawi's translator renders it—was a popular form of entertainment at the time.]

let us not forget that he translated from Syriac,[2] not from Greek, so it is possible that the misunderstanding of Aristotle's book began with the Syriac translator.[3]

In *Sternstunden der Menschheit* [Decisive Moments in History], the Austrian writer Stefan Zweig recounts historical events that may seem trivial in themselves, but that had very important consequences. For example, shortly before the battle of Waterloo, Napoleon was waiting for aid from one of his officers, but the latter lost his way and did not arrive at the battlefield until the matter was concluded and the emperor had been defeated. Thus the face of Europe changed because of something silly, an officer who lost his way. Perhaps we could add to the fateful hours that Stefan Zweig relates the one in which Matta ibn Yunus translated Aristotle's *Poetics* into Arabic.

It is amusing to recall what 'Abd al-Rahman Badawi wrote in this regard: "It seems to us that if this book, Aristotle's *Poetics*, were understood correctly, and its subjects, views, and principles implemented, Arabic literature would have incorporated the higher poetic genres, tragedy and comedy, from the age of its flowering in the third century of the *hijrah* [ninth century A.D.] onward, and the whole face of Arabic literature would have

2. This is what Abu Said al-Sirafi faulted him for in the famous debate that took place between them: "You do not, then, invite us to the study of logic, you invite us to learn the Greek language, which you do not know. How can you want us to learn a language that you have not learned? You translate from Syriac; what do you say about meanings that change when translated from Greek into Syriac, then from Syriac into Arabic?" (al-Tawhidi n.d., 1: 111).

3. On the Syriac translation, of which only a few lines are extant, see Wolfhart Heinrichs, *Arabische Dichtung und griechische Poetik* [1969], 112–18.

changed" (Badawi 1973, 56). Arabic literature, then, lacks the higher poetic genres, and from this perspective, it is inevitably deficient. Apparently, this would not have happened if the *Poetics* had been translated properly and faithfully; had Matta ibn Yunus not failed in his translation, the face of Arabic literature would have changed. It ought to have changed, yet unfortunately it remained the same for a trivial reason, an error that could have been avoided.

In this way, with a pen stroke—a bitter pen that knows no irony—ten centuries of Arabic literature are written off. But that is not enough for Badawi, who adds, "Who knows! Perhaps the face of Arab civilization as a whole would have changed with its literature, as Europe changed in the Renaissance!" (56). The face of Arabic literature, the face of Arab civilization: that face was nearly disfigured and erased; the Arabs almost lost their identity and their Arabness and became Europeans. Indeed, they almost became Europeans before the fact, before the Europeans! If the latter achieved their renaissance starting from the fifteenth century, Arabs could have achieved that same renaissance in the ninth century, that is, six centuries before the Europeans.

If we follow this idea to its logical conclusion, we would arrive at the following: had the Arabs understood the *Poetics* properly, there would have been no need for the European Renaissance. Why would the Europeans undertake a renaissance that the Arabs had already achieved? Europeans would have simply woken up one day to find that the Arabs had achieved the renaissance centuries earlier; that being the case, they would have had no choice but to imitate them and learn from them. Thus, Matta's atrocious translation was disastrous not only for the Arabs because it prevented them from becoming European, but also for the Europeans because it delayed their renaissance by several centuries. All of this happened because of two words, on the understanding of which the fate of the world depended.

But why not say that the Arabs owe Matta ibn Yunus a great debt? Perhaps he saved them, through his bad translation, from a great danger that threatened them. Had it not been for him, they would have left behind the literary genres and norms to which they were accustomed, and studied Greek literature with the intention of imitating it. Thanks to Matta ibn Yunus and his unfaithful translation, Arabs were able to go on believing that their poetry is the poetry and their language the language. This translator saved them unintentionally, accidentally, and unwittingly.

Unwittingly? Did he really misunderstand what Aristotle meant by "tragedy" and "comedy"? Who knows! Perhaps he was fully aware of their meaning, and perhaps he deliberately rendered them as panegyric and satire for some undisclosed reason![4]

This can never be verified. What is certain is that Matta did not know that over the centuries something would change in the world, and that Arabs would one day need to translate others' literatures and to speak other languages besides theirs.

4. This hypothesis would make a good subject for a novel.

Works Cited

Abu al-Anwar, Muhammad. 1981. *Mustafa Lutfi al-Manfaluti: Hayatuh wa adabuh.* Cairo: Maktabat al-shabab.

Allen, Roger, and D. S. Richards, eds. 2006. *Arabic Literature in the Post-Classical Period.* Cambridge: Cambridge Univ. Press.

Amireh, Amal. 2002. "Framing Nawal El-Saadawi: Arab Feminism in a Transnational World." In *Intersections: Gender, Nation, and Community in Arab Women's Novels,* edited by Lisa Suhair Majaj, Paula W. Sunderman, and Therese Saliba, 33–67. Syracuse: Syracuse Univ. Press.

Amireh, Amal, and Lisa Suhair Majaj, eds. 2000. *Going Global: The Transnational Reception of Third World Women Writers.* New York: Garland.

Apter, Emily. 2006. *The Translation Zone: A New Comparative Literature.* Princeton: Princeton Univ. Press.

Aristotle. 1973. *Fan al-shiʻr.* Edited and translated into Arabic by ʻAbd al-Rahman Badawi. Beirut: Dar al-thaqafah.

Badawi, ʻAbd al-Rahman. 1973. "Tasdir ʻam." In Aristotle, *Fan al-shiʻr.* Edited and translated into Arabic by ʻAbd al-Rahman Badawi. Beirut: Dar al-thaqafah. 11–56.

Benjamin, Walter. 1968. "The Task of the Translator." *Illuminations: Essays and Reflections.* Translated by Harry Zohn. New York: Schocken Books.

Birge-Vitz, Evelyn. 1975. "Type et individu dans l'autobiographie médiévale." *Poétique* 24: 426–45.

Borges, Jorge Luis. 1998. "Averroës' Search." *Collected Fictions.* Translated by Andrew Hurley. New York: Penguin.

Butterworth, Charles E. 1986. Preface to Ibn Rushd, *Averroes' Middle Commentary on Aristotle's Poetics*, ix–xvi. Translated by Charles Butterworth. Princeton: Princeton Univ. Press.

Dante. 1954. *The Divine Comedy*. Translated by H. R. Huse. New York: Holt, Rinehart and Winston.

De Man, Paul. 1986. *The Resistance to Theory*. Minneapolis: Univ. of Minnesota Press.

Dunn, Ross E. 1986. *The Adventures of Ibn Battuta*. Berkeley: Univ. of California Press.

Al-Halabi, Ali Hassan Ali, Ibrahim Taha Qaysi, and Hamdi Muhammad Murad. 1999. *Mawsu'at al-ahadith wa al-athar al-da'ifa wa al-mawdu'a*. Riyadh: Maktabat al-ma'arif li al-nashr wa al-tawzi'.

Hassan, Waïl S. 2006. "Agency and Translational Literature: Ahdaf Soueif's *The Map of Love*." *PMLA* 121, no. 3 (May): 753–68.

Heinrichs, Wolfhart. 1969. *Arabische Dichtung und griechische Poetik*. Beirut: Orient-Institut der Deutschen Morgenländischen Gesellschaft.

Ibn Battuta. 1958–2000. *The Travels of Ibn Battuta*. 5 vols. Translated by H.A.R. Gibb. Cambridge: Cambridge Univ. Press.

Ibn Rushd. 1986. *Averroes' Middle Commentary on Aristotle's Poetics*. Translated by Charles Butterworth. Princeton: Princeton Univ. Press.

Al-Jahiz. 1996. *Kitab al-hayawan*. Edited by 'Abd al-Salam Muhammad Harun. Beirut: Dar al-Jil.

———. N.d. *Kitab al-bayan wa al-tabyyin*. Edited by 'Abd al-Salam Muhammad Harun. Beirut: Dar al-Jil.

Kahf, Mohja. 2000. "Packaging Huda Sha'rawi's Memoirs in the United States Reception Environment." In *Going Global: The Transnational Reception of Third World Women Writers*, edited by Amal Amireh and Lisa Suhair Majaj, 148–72. New York: Garland.

Khatibi, Abdelkébir. 1983. *L'amour bilingue*. Paris: Fata Morgana. In English, *Love in Two Languages*. Translated by Richard Howard. Minneapolis: Univ. of Minnesota Press, 1990.

Kelly, Robert, Jacques Roubaud, and [Francis Picabia] Schuldt. 1995. *Abziehbilder, heimgeholt.* Graz-Wien: Literaturverlag Droschl.

Kilito, Abdelfattah. 1983. *Les séances: Récits et codes culturels chez Hamadhanî et Harîrî.* Paris: Sindbad. In Arabic, *Al-maqamat.* Translated by Abd al-Kabir al-Sharqawi. Casablanca: Dar Toubkal, 1993.

———. 1999. "Borges et Averroès." *Horizons maghrébins* 41: 13–16.

———. 2001. *The Author and His Doubles: Essays on Classical Arabic Culture.* Translated by Michael Cooperson. Syracuse: Syracuse Univ. Press.

Laroui, Abdallah. 1977. *Les origines sociales et culturelles du nationalisme marocain.* Paris: F. Maspero.

Leon, Donna. 1992. *Death at La Fenice.* New York: HarperCollins.

Majaj, Lisa Suhair, Paula W. Sunderman, and Therese Saliba, eds. 2002. *Intersections: Gender, Nation, and Community in Arab Women's Novels.* Syracuse: Syracuse Univ. Press.

Miller, Susan Gilson. 1992. Introduction to Muhammad as-Saffar, *Disorienting Encounters: Travels of a Moroccan Scholar in France in 1845–1846. The Voyage of Muhammad As-Saffar,* 3–69. Edited and translated by Susan Gilson Miller. Berkeley: Univ. of California Press.

Pellat, Charles. 1953. *Le milieu basrien et la formation de Jâhiz.* Paris: Adrien-Maisonneuve.

———. 1970. *Langue et littérature arabes.* 2nd ed. Paris: Armand Colin.

The Qur'an. 2004. Translated by M. A. S. Abdel Haleem. Oxford: Oxford Univ. Press.

Renan, Ernest. 1997. *Averroès et l'averroïsme.* Paris: Maisonneuve et Larose.

Robinson, Douglas. 1996. *Translation and Taboo.* DeKalb: Northern Illinois Univ. Press.

As-Saffar, Muhammad. 1992. *Disorienting Encounters: Travels of a Moroccan Scholar in France in 1845–1846. The Voyage of*

Muhammad As-Saffar. Edited and translated by Susan Gilson Miller. Berkeley: Univ. of California Press.

Shammas, Anton. 1988. *Arabesques*. Translated by Vivian Eden. New York: Harper and Row.

Al-Shidyaq, Ahmad Faris. 1920. *Al-saq ʿala al-saq fi ma huwa al-Fariyaq*. Cairo: Al-maktabah al-jadidah.

———. 1867. *Kitab al-rihlah al-mawsumah bi al-wasita ila maʿrifat malta wa kashf al-mukhabba ʿan funun urubba*. Tunis: Al-matbaʿa al-tunissiya.

Siddiq, Muhammad. 2000. "Al-kitaba bi al-ʿibriyya al-fusha: Taqdim riwayat ʿarabisk wa hiwar maʿa Anton Shammas." *Alif: Journal of Comparative Poetics* 20: 155–67.

Spivak, Gayatri Chakravorty. 1993. "The Politics of Translation." *Outside in the Teaching Machine*. New York: Routledge.

Al-Tabari, Abu Jaʿfar Muhammad ibn Jarir. 1984. *Jamiʿ al-bayan ʿan taʾwil ay al-qurʾan*. 15 vols. Beirut: Dar al-fikr.

Al-Tahtawi, Rifaʿa Rafiʿ. 1834/2004. *An Imam in Paris: Account of a Stay in France by an Egyptian Cleric (1826–1831) (Takhlis al-ibriz fi talkhis bariz aw al-diwan al-nafis bi-iwan baris)*. Translated by Daniel L. Newman. London: Saqi.

Al-Tawhidi, Abu Hayyan. N.d. *Al-imtaʿ wa al-muʾanasa*. Edited by Ahmad Amin and Ahmad al-Zayn. Beirut: Dal al-Hayah.

Webster's New World Dictionary. 1988. 3rd collegiate edition. Cleveland: Webster's New World.

Zweig, Stefan. 1962. *Sternstunden der Menschheit*. Frankfurt: Verlag. In English, *Decisive Moments in History*. Translated by Lowell A. Bangerter. Riverside, Calif.: Ariadne Press, 1999.